SELECTED POEMS

Ben Mazer

MADHAT PRESS
ASHEVILLE, NORTH CAROLINA

MadHat Press
MadHat Incorporated
PO Box 8364, Asheville, NC 28814

The Library of Congress has assigned
this edition a Control Number of
2017913592

ISBN 978-1-941196-58-8 (paperback)

All deviations from conventional spelling and punctuation
are deliberate aesthetic choices by the author

Text by Ben Mazer
Cover photograph by Ciprian Hord
Cover design by Marc Vincenz

www.MadHat-Press.com

First Printing

SELECTED POEMS

To Stephen Sturgeon

A Preface to Ben Mazer
by Philip Nikolayev

Vladimir Nabokov, in his novel *Transparent Things,* speaks of physical objects that appear sheer to the gifted perceiver, their entire individual histories visible through them. In Ben Mazer's poetry, everything and everyone seems to display a similar quality at moments of heightened, transcendent perception, when the world (or possibly the brain: it's debatable) begins to pulse freely to its inherent musical rhythm, dictating visions and verses. In order to realize its own truth, the present—the place in the moment, with living people in it—must be able to perceive itself (through the poet's mind, whose else?) as a singing, lyric entity that is exactly such as it is because of how the past has mingled with the leaves and the stars and the clouds and the shingle boards of the ancient house of the present—things transient and eternal—as well as with the ghostly presences of the dead and with all that dark and imperfectly understood stuff that that both holds us together and constantly challenges us as a species. The lyric moment is simultaneously musical and paradoxical.

Such are the energies that fuel a particular kind of lyric beauty, the kind that informs much of the writing in this uniquely important volume. The poet acts here as the oracle—sometimes perhaps as the trickster god—of that special perceptual state. The material is beauty, inseparable from love and sadness, the stuff of metaphor, but the paradoxical form of expression often points to a metaphysical depth in the poems. The variety of tone is most welcome. The speaker—the lyric character of these dramatic monologs—is fixed yet protean, like a god. That's what we may call the Ben Mazer lyric trick. Logically, it seems impossible to be both fixed and ever changing—a paradox. But things needn't seem to be logically possible to be possible, or real for that matter. Does the universe seem to be logically possible? Does the brain? Search Einstein.

Like the universe, humans embody and thus to some extent resolve apparent contradictions. The poet is, ideally, the most human of mortals, poetry being, ideally, the distilled, well-formed and well-reflected expression of humanity, of human perception and self-perception. Poetry draws our attention to observations that are by and large indifferent to philosophy because they are insufficiently general; yet they may well be of cognitive interest because they mirror something of how thoughtful perception works on a day-to-day basis, constantly moving between paradox and resolution. For our purposes, to resolve a paradox is simply to understand its truth, overcoming an initial disbelief. At first chime, a statement like "All is statistics, with a fudge sundae sealed"—a line of Mazer's—has a bizarre ring to it, yet on reflection it turns out to be a true assertion and not difficult to accept. The result of putting it this way is a renewed perception, a fresh angle on the familiar, in the given context.

The lyric character assumes many guises, enters into various narrative situations, some more fantastical than others, speaking in the first person, the second, or the third. He often identifies with a marginal, sketchy figure who nevertheless has more than meets the naked eye to recommend him. He has special knowhow and privileged insights. Now he is a traveller, anonymous and haunted by a problematic past, "in a strange country"; now a jailbird leading a prison break; then a spy in exile, "handled by the handler's handler" in an attractive mountain village with a faintly European feel (are there villages in the U.S.?), who finds himself reading the local newspaper backwards, presumably for secret code, and winds up experiencing a wild banquet as a vision of a mass descent into hell; and then again he speaks as a Welsh king, alienated but coming to grips with his hereditary royalty, his "divine rights." Court and courtship, high expectations and high standards of sentiment and decorum, manifest themselves, not without a delicious irony, in this body of sophisticated yet moving 21st-century verse, much of which has an adventurist, experimental edge to it. Much of the time, too, the speaker is recognizably the poet Ben Mazer of Harvard Square and vicinity. It all coheres, the product of one large, peculiar mind.

As is natural for a lyric, unabashedly Romantic poet of Mazer's kidney, love is central to his affairs and projects—love unrequited and love fulfilled, the couple in love and the love triangle, love betrayed, love hopeful, the subtle politics and anxieties of love—along with other forms of affection, such as friendship and spiritual kinship. Mazer's standards in this sphere are a poet's: chivalric, quixotic, and uncompromising. "Only true love can influence the warden," remarks he, and elsewhere: "True friendship survives the time it learned to kill." These are lines that matter, their echoes travel far in the imagination. The poet is a master of feeling, he knows how to evaluate the truth and worth of a sentiment.

In the poems, feelings often come into play at symbolically significant locales suggestive or royalty and aristocracy. Mazer's lyric character gives the impression of fancying things that are old school, secrets nearly extinct, wines of distinguished vintage (though the poet himself doesn't drink), fine cigars, objects and people aglow with their own histories. He adores the palace, the castle, the ancestral manor, the garden, the tower, and similarly imposing, traditionally prized locales, whether gothically landscaped and architected or evocative of "British wishes." Mazer exhibits a pre-postmodern lack of disdain for the precious. In a world seen as gentlefolk's noble consensus, but verified by the poet's well-attuned intuition, a coat of arms, for example, may serve to represent the idea of an unapologetically old-fashioned, aesthetically motivated code of honor. Both have a certain museum quality to them, 'like they don't make any more', as it is said. It stands to reason that such poetic imagery has nothing to do with the idealization of any aristocratic or other historical social class.

Any idyllic symmetries that may be insinuated by the high-end venues and landscapes that Mazer favors and employs as needed, are mercilessly challenged by the pressures of passionate experience, the serial comedies and tragedies of life. The candid emotional spontaneity of much of Mazer's verse, its primal givenness to tears and laughter, vibrates through the masterful indirection (and occasional blunt, disarming directness) of expression, betraying the great vulnerability and resilience of the generous heart that throbs in the lines, spilling over. Fill your cups!

CONTENTS

The Glass Piano (2015)

WHITE CITIES (1995)

A VISITOR

The flier, at the Wicklow manor,
Stayed throughout the spring and summer,
Mending autos in the drive,
Reprising time-old moods of love
In the limbs of country lasses
Who wondered where he gave his kisses.

Expert at geography
And mathematic, for no fee
He made the summer days pass faster
And taught them how to see the pasture
With their own eyes. The books he read,
Handled till their cloth was frayed,
Years afterwards upon their shelves
Lay early, central to their lives.

A Traveller

In a strange country, there is only one
Who knows his true name and could turn him in.
But she, whose father too was charged with murder
And, innocent, went to the electric chair,
Believes in him, convinces him to trust.
It is the tropics where they make their tryst.
They sip refreshing drinks beside a terraced
Pool where he is thought to be a tourist.
To clear his name, and find who killed his pal,
In a dark passage he finds hope and will.
What once had seemed exotic now seems near
Because he wished to be her prisoner.

Hospital Song

Back from the wars,
Without my wares,
But lying here,
Not quite sure where,
Permitted this,
Calm to the eyes,
A world of shadow,
Suited for widow.

Burnt smells no longer
In nostrils linger,
Yet others attack,
Slightly septic;
Difference is
Most wise of laws
And here no hurry,
But sanctuary.

POEMS (2010)

The Double

I remember chiefly the warp of the curb, and time going by.
As time goes by. I remember red gray green blue brown brick
before rain or during rain. One doesn't see who is going by.
One doesn't think to see who is going by.
One sees who is going by all right, but one doesn't see who is
        going by.
The bright lights attract customers to the bookstore.
Seeing, chalk it up to that. The bitter looks of the booksellers,
as you leave the shop without paying. Rickety steps that will
        soon
be history. A ripped up paperback book with some
        intelligent inscriptions
in very dried out blue gray ink. Lots of dumpsters. And seagulls.
Or are they pigeons. They seem related, as the air is to the sea.
When it gets darker, or foggier, it is a really big soup
of souls, works of art, time tables, the hour before dinner,
theatrical enterprise, memories of things never happened,
        warnings
spoken in a voice familiar, a keen and quickened sense
of possibility glimpsed through windows.
Handbills, whatever to mark the passing time. And sleep.
I know it is good when the good of it is not noticed.
It is something you try to tell someone privately in a room
where the light is broken in October. Your sense of time
is the source of your charm with strangers,
who would accept you anyways.
Nora Laudani was the best actress in our elementary school.
One felt she was a great lady at seventeen.
The tragic view of ice skating frightens us
at night in winter. In a soup you never know

what you'll run into next. All the ingredients repeat,
but you encounter some of them for the first time. Strangers
turn out to be people you know later on. Sometimes even
        dead people's
lives are only a stone's throw away from your own. First you
        heard of them,
or heard someone speaking like them. Generations of birds
are some kind of commentary on it. People who moved out
        precede you.
If your cousins are playing football on the lawn, then
        somebody else's cousins
played football on the lawn. You try to imagine them when
        you are alone.
It is interesting that you are the only one on the street. Time
        as a movie.
When you are walking everything is moving. It kind of
        reaches out at you,
as if inviting you to stop and visit with it,
as if having a particular story to tell.
You can't keep your mind on the story it has to tell.
But some of the things you're reminded of *are* the story it's
        telling you.
They are too much like other things you've heard about.
        Their advantage is
the hands of trees think you want to pick them. They kind
        of don't want you to go inside,
but they want you to know that something's going on in there.
I am constantly reminded of George Washington
when I look in at the shapes of windows. Social courtesy
        looms large,

and throws lavish parties. Its savage powers are pride's poster.
There is a kind of perpetual removal in a spiral.
The case of a person who is very rapidly assessing several
    objects at once.
He either has a machine to do this for him, or recognizes value.
I was thinking of the moon along the Wabash.
In April white scroll-work admires magnolias.
The white picket fence is and has always been intense.
After a while Walt Whitman doesn't come again, but is in
    fact receding.
Snow has a very conspiratorial hush in circumstances similar
    to these.
One lets a real good laugh out. The universe seems to yield a
    little bit for the laugh.
The stars pass the houses more quickly than you do.
Your race is the measure of time.
Your race is the meaning of time.
That makes you laugh. After all it looks like it is just you
and pavement that is going nowhere. The houses in back lots
    between houses
raise their hats in your hopes until you see them as dead wood,
and begin to get thoughts related to the inception of maps.
This's binary coordinate is sleep.
Often it is much better than I am describing.
Now let it be a lens through which we look at the city
on a long drive at night, with its feeling of going to a doctor.
Shy shared moments between the wind and the palmetto,
and a feeling of having been missed by only ten or twenty years.
Something which is not wholly love and only abstractly
    journalism.

In the luggage department palmettos are on empty. The steps
are your best bet. Try prickly! Past the doorbell
lies the paradise for which you are kicking yourself.

Rhapsody on a Winter Night

The closed world adumbrates the snow.
Midnight deciphers pillows at the window.
Though it was several months ago,
in dead of winter, nothing knows or shows
where the requested intimacy goes.
The silent isolated frames
of meditation have dispersed with names.
The couches crouch in feeble poses,
incognizant of roses.

Ben Mazer

DEATH AND MINSTRELSY

*Our references have all aged a little
as we were looking at them, not noticing.*
—John Ashbery

That hulking rooftop like a leviathan
still unexpectedly sails into view,
its byzantine tilework faded red and grey
like boxes within boxes visible from the sea,
at summer's start eluding the goswogii.
Woodberry's copy of his life of Poe
emerges from the flood, a constancy
that nobody will buy year after year.
Poe was born in Boston. In aught nine
Bruce Rogers did the job and Eliot
did shameful things that never will be known
on out of town trips. Something in the fog
grins like a skeleton beneath the cracked
continuity of what seemed like time.
Fall is spring-like. The fresh violins
of new arrangements lift the tortured heart
to hope, reflected light, the heart laid bare.
Poems are but evidence of poetry.
Mysterious kitchens you shall search them all—
and choose your death at sea by thirty-three.
And once in winter heard the Archduke Trio
performed by friends in the conservatory.
Although I am only a moderate admirer
of your poetry, there is not a single other
contemporary poet who I do admire.
The museum closes in a timeless wave
of unutterable rhythms, lashed by rain.

14

The sea's maw beckons to the life it spawned.
The white sheen of a sun pierced spray of fog
as we drop down the hill to the cliff's edge
pierces the crowd out of time's slow parade
that hits us like old music or a dream,
billowing out between their stupored legs,
the hot dog zeppelins and powder flags,
as if unseeable, but the grey ghost
of that hellion rowing with an iron crowbar
peers out through banjo chinks in the ragtime
that's near but sounds as if it's far away,
the certainty of death past the breakers.

THE LONG WHARF

It takes awhile to walk through the long wharf
which is enclosed against the elements.
Purveying the connecting properties
to the new lease, our party sauntered there,
in the bright glare of light deflecting night,
the Chinaman, the Frenchman and the Swede
(each in a pressed suit, just off an airplane,
and eager to get back to the hotel,
to sink in privacy into a drink
in a bright glare of light deflecting night),
their uninformed eyes taking little care
(the tour was peppered with such agent's talk
as never hesitates in its intent,
was not designed for one to really look),
while the collector of fine bric-a-brac
who counted millions in the warehoused goods
rubbed off a bit of calculating pride
on objects he could not commit to sell,
stealthy foundations of his capital:
each type of bottle from each type of year,
each printed calendar that was produced,
all manufactured products, everything
preserved unopened in its packaging
just as it was when joie de vivre was king
(the Englishwoman served him to this end,
looking upon him as upon a friend).
The long wharf was unstable in the wind.
We didn't realize it was a wharf
we had come through, but at the end of it
a weather-rotted window peered out on

the ocean, we could see how far we'd come
held up above the sea by massive beams,
a long way out, and swaying in the wind
with little place to walk on the loose floor.

I thought of falling out into the sea.
The ocean is blue, but many shades of blue
and white and green, and black and grey, combined
in motion, rising towards us on a page
behind which light hides echoes of nothing.
Nothing is all we know of what is there.
It seems so heavy, heavier than dreams,
as deep as dreams would ever think to go,
in the black murky movement that's not there.
What ever comes behind has come before
and either is or has or hasn't been,
it's not for us to say. If we're not here,
historically, life is happening elsewhere.
All is a paradigm, the diver's bow
is nothing if not everything we know.
I want to turn the page. I am afraid
of what is out there, the horizon, ships—
depthless darkness, uncertain vantages.
I pulled back from the wind as from a nail,
and turned to go. There on some long tables
(I had been squeezed between them and the wall
when I had had my vision of my fall)
whose sides were built up so that they were bins,
I saw enormous quantities of slips
of paper, very thin, filed in long rows.

I opened one to see what slips they were.
Upon each one, and now I saw the ships
that must have been as real as you or I,
the name recorded of each voyager
transgressing the horizon on a ship
who entered here, each entry had a slip—
a continent of ghosts had landed here,
thick on the tables, only the fog moved
and the long wharf stayed up and swayed in place.

Second Rhapsody on a Winter Night [Variations on a Winter Night]

I

Night extends opacities
of being and of consciousness.
Physical vacuities.

Beneath the porcelain awake
tidal waves of other lives
and unburied memory.

The evening hour's to and fro,
time's thick repercussions bloom
(the hour of the small meeting).

Landscape and emotion rains.
Consciousness and being drains.
And toy soldiers storm the seas.

II

Tangled prospects of the trees.
Perspectives' difficulties.

Scenery that no one sees.
Perpetual vacuities.

Amid it all an ancient roar,
a disciplinary whisper.

A confidence of alcoves,
a confidence of loves.

And the disconnected spires,
and the disembodied towers.

The splintered multiplicity
of bare branches of a tree.
Scenery that no one sees.
The row of deserted balconies.
(A light comes on between the trees
and flickers from within a room.)
The tangled vacuities
of shade and shape
of shape and shade.
The tomorrow that's prepared.

Footprints through pure forms of snow
sink like thought into shadow.
Snow that's piled on barriers,
motionless fragments of verse.

And the soul shrinks in the wood
far from what is understood.

(The lights come on between the trees.)

And the toy soldiers storm the seas.

Tangled prospects of the trees.
Perspectives' difficulties.

And the sleeping melodies
of motionless uncertainties.
And the sleeping melodies
of abandoned vacancies.
And the sleeping melodies
of forms and structures without cease.
And the sleeping melodies
of abandoned centuries.
And the streetlight on the street,
the absent tread of absent feet.

And the soul shrinks in the wood
far from what is understood.

(And flickers from within a room
where I shall neither go nor come.)
The bold indifference of the moon
settles on a window pane.
And tomorrow is prepared
in the darkness without word.
As darkness with symphonic form
agitates the empty room.
As stillness with symphonic form
agitates the lifeless room.
And tomorrow is prepared
in the hall without a sound.
Wordlessly as memory.

Wordlessly as memory
through the outer room is wound.
(The present and the future bound.)
As silence with symphonic form
agitates the sleepless room.
And tomorrow is prepared.
And tomorrow is prepared,
and the future is secured
(though the present is obscured).
And the world itself is tired.
Language by itself is bored.
And tomorrow is required.
And the morning is prepared.

Consciousness and being drains.
Landscape and emotion rains.

Ancestral resonances freeze.
And the toy soldiers storm the seas.

THE EXILE

I was handled by the handler's handler
someone (I know who) had sent me to.
A mountain zephyr blew the sunlight cold.
I read the little village paper backwards
and nibbled at my ham. Coffee is birth.
I was surprised to see how things had changed
since I first dreamed I came here long ago.
The villagers were lobbying new plans,
who had been immigrants before the snow.
I was among the first to try the new
cuisine, the classless restaurant.
In the best house I recognized my host,
and he who had fulfilled a noble life
exhibited no need for conversation.
Then I was swept up in the exultation
of thousands of revelers' descent to hell.

ORIENT HEIGHTS

Orient heights the sole star blessed
motion against motion movement against movement
to the one house buried in the rest
no one sees me but an old man
I've come to use drunk in his playroom
sole star blessed and a blank page
divided between the world as we know it
the world as we saw it and a blank page
and all the rest Orient heights

While You Were Watching Richard Harris

Then or now, the eye let on the storm.
Winks of knowing, dead before alive.
Simple patter, nothing to write home.
British wishes, twentieth century jive.

An ape's greek profile, and the grainy slosh
of primary dimensions. Tragedy
is just a face, enslavement's kitchenette.
This has the mortal sound of tragic ease.

The awkward awful listenerless blown
enjambments. Dreadful paraphrase. Unshown!
Escapes amazement. Notches on recall
the figurement of the Platonic wall.

Yet, lacking mores, nothing to exhume.
As if from rooftops lengthening to bloom.

Ben Mazer

Before Us

in memoriam Frank Parker

Lowell winning the Pulitzer in 1947 ...
Pushing ecstatic through the darkening crowd ...
the newspapers not yet lifted, fish and corn
wrapped by the flashing grocer, millennial ...
weighed in two scales by his hurt, flashing eyes ...
a seething margin, bustling with friends
and lovers, trinket-shaking sky, to die ...
how can they tell us what they didn't know?
Logical types the century pressed white ...
rounding the corner of each first familiar
tombstone or commemorative stone
cut in the image of the training sailor ...
homecoming, whether on the edge of home.
Writing is fighting in the Christ-whale's eyes.

The Big House

Spring draws archival colors, brief and brittle
as celluloid, its technicolor process
too early for man, too late for a bright rebuttal,
along dirt roads, easing out travellers' faces.
Love swings in gates, shines in new coats of white,
tuning up breezes, whistling branches and collars,
lighting out birds, examining concrete
as far as the eye can see, exploding flowers.
Bringing petitions for a timely pardon,
willing to go on record if it might save,
only true love can influence the warden.
"I'm giving the orders now. We're crashing out."
Living the rest of my days the way he might have,
out of the prison now, I'll write about it.

Evening

Coming in the vastly later
like a time we had prepared
as if the stars invented dinner
or the evening had been cleared
by sheer invention of another
long before the deal was queered
we stepped into the times of tables
and the primes of motor cars
waiting for us as in fables
under the invented stars
and the transience of those times
were intimately just for us
a resurrection history climbs
to catch an after dinner bus
while some absent early other
shone to rankle and to bother.

A Movie Is Available Knowledge

A movie is available knowledge,
interdisciplinary garb, insane voice
uttering knowledge. Too much fun
remembers. On the hill the balcony
is windy. Better be said. Nothing
recommends the bluebirds. Better
the west wind. Remembers the ghosts love.
I am troubled by experience.

The high hedges languish the ocean.
Here it is eves then. Notion
knows no no. The North Star
freezes the ship's light like fire
over the white surf. The black death
roars silence, over the white sands.

TONGA

Out by the international dateline
where time begins in the earth's atmosphere
as far as can be from any mainland
surrounded by ocean to the southern pole
it's dizzying to catch the ocean breeze
and dizzying to speak with the natives
who are hemmed in without a newspaper
except what we deliver through the air
from Honolulu or Australia
(it's difficult for aircraft just to land
on such a slender strip you might have missed
patrolling vast unrecognizable
wastelands of ocean in a linear motion,
not mentioning there's no place to refuel
beyond Vanuatu or Kiribati,
the Marshall Islands falling in the sea)
and dizzying turned under from the sun
where even satellites refuse to go
and post their differentials to the moon;
we're upside down here, settling into talk
among the grasses, the colonial palace
of the last uncolonized monarchy,
there's tea for you, and tea for me,
and passports for a bindle of currency;
cultural gifts that few will get to see
are removed to the palace of the old king
his friend, his police captain, and his spokesman
is missing at golf, and won't be here today,
making his rounds of confiscations
protecting citizens under the new bill

just last week passed and signed by the old king
permitting no anti-government journalism
no freedom of the press (where we come in,
launching our cutting edge of poetry
like fresh air to selected citizens;
we're going to mount our reputations here
on this quelled insulated friendly isle
friendly to transport of Al-Queda warheads
they didn't know their boats were carrying;
how many international criminals
have found discreet peace here, new identities,
allowing them to contribute to the culture
in little ways, by sponsoring brisk teas
where they respect the monarch's aging wishes
and find a little chore or two to do,
mostly to keep things running pretty smoothly
among the known world's highest literacy
where Tongan, Tongan, Tongan reigns supreme
down to the water, the corrugated shacks
hungry for poetry news from Cambridge, Mass.;
it's dizzying, dizzying, to be cast so far
from any other mainland, closer to the moon
in understanding intersubjectivity.
You tilt the globe to see how far it is
it might fall off, be swept over, or forgotten,
but the monarch has been rich for fifty years,
he's old and stoops, observing with dark shades
his little military exercises
performed with a quaint and pre-Edwardian feel
rag tag as demonstrations in Vancouver

when the English Queen was visiting;
Oh Tonga, Tonga, by your lights no leave
gives me no hope to buy the government,
install myself as king in quiet peace,
for the king is old, must be approaching death,
though his old flunkeys never think of it.
Tonga, Tonga, it's so dizzying
receiving odd supplies from Honolulu
Havana of the west, Pacific haven
for adventurers who've lost their names
but fit in with the slow and daily pace
of the monarch's generosity
I want to live there, far from continents,
close to the dizzying moon and southern pole
where day begins for all the certain earth's
trust in firm numbers, nothing to the sea,
dizzying, dizzying, ready to collapse
from an unvetted critical intrusion,
from Yale's designs to instigate confusion
and spread the latest word to promulgate
incendiary interests on their dripping peace.
So dizzy, dizzy, underneath the world,
spread like a picnic on the ocean,
unrecognizable on any map
on google global or atlas msn,
lost as moon craters or a speck of dust,
hanging upside down in primitive lust
communal and untouchable their ports
the daily delivery by air inspected
for just the sort of cosmopolitan

eastern propaganda, capital
the monarch confiscates or highly taxes
until my surreptitious operation
enlists approval from the CIA
within the bounds of international law
subjected to the monarch's scrutiny;
where nothing escapes the notice of the king.
Oh Tonga Tonga, dizzying education
in primitive charm and ancient rituals
ordained by the half-century's monarchy
at last I'll make my exit to the moon
and touch down in the sub-tropical waters
where no one can find me, where I can't even breathe
so rarefied the air swept by the ocean
outside surveillance, beyond the calendar,
like upside down boxes of cereal
I empty on the table, too proud to eat,
marvelling at the direction through earth's center
that leads me to the silent peace of Tonga.
No longer on any map, I'll be myself.
A wise man with an ivy education,
a friend to primitives and government,
advisor to the bankers and the flunkeys
who are the same, in need of better speeches.
So Tonga bring me in, a secret weapon
to increase trade and visibility,
to edit a respectful local paper
with news of the outside world and cutting culture
that cannot hurt the monarch's steady grip
on the compliance of his faithful subjects

but do not hack my emails in the east,
Tonga is mine, the dizzying atmosphere
is what I seek, quite far from any mainland,
adrift in the ocean nearer the southern pole
indifferent to testings on the Marshall Islands
where I shall sit beneath a breadfruit tree
counting the minutes of imagination
and testing the mails to see what can get through
supplies to print my kind of newspaper
which I'll distribute hoping to be king
after researching the better addresses
of my potential allies among the people.
No spyplanes and no spying satellites
will know what I am doing, in the skies
I see reflections of an endless sea
which I maintain shall all belong to me
no matter if the air grows somewhat thin
and coastlines crumble where I make my fortune,
as close to outer space as earth can be.

THE PEGASII

Sunlight rests like a package at the door.
Nothing sees. The rich interior
is useless to persons and chronology.
Once when the spring came to our caravan
I'd say the mountain streams ran in her hair.
Let these things rest without a memory.

THE GHOSTS

Immediately finding themselves dead,
above their fallen bodies
the ghosts watch with astonishment and rage
to see the evening through a lens of fire
as friends and lovers in a strange parade
pass not hearing. Love's own ground
is patient in eternity. The proof
of love is hidden, but familiar.
It was as fresh as spring, in the old life.
To have no idea of the coming change.
Not long ago, the climate's urgencies
sped them to silence. A sense of hope
is what lingers. Each counterpart of ghosts
relives serenity, the daily puzzle
of shadow on shadow, smiles unwinding talk
where everything happens, as proof exists.
How could they have known what it was like?
The violence of a ghost disarranging books.

SAN FRANCISCO POEMS

I

HOMAGE TO CALIFORNIA

He built his home up on the glittering hill.
I wanted to own the earth. Dear—
I have been struggling a lot
lately with the meaning of my life.
Twenty years later in the history of the world
I return to *languid mysteriousness,*
night blooming jasmine—the scene of this
my youth I had forgotten (ledge)
and the deep darkness of the brightest star—
I swear I remember impossible alcoves
I came up once where the secluding vines
and oriental gardens knew my mind,
in the first days of being steeped in wine.
I loved then. I love now. Love is the same.
It is not possible to love enough
the distant sweetness of this paradise.
Like a museum is the life I watch—
no one can hear me now or see me now—
Aliki Barnstone Ted Walther George Hitchcock
my roommate John and Lawrence who is dead
the ring of dancers circling through the wood
is broken. Forever time begins again.
Life is different. Nothing is the same.
My life is waste. I wanted to own the earth.

Shut out of the twentieth century—
you cannot hear a one of these pressed flowers.
Everything I love spells ALCATRAZ

The headlight through pine needles. The first glimpse
at the bronze lawn piece of the chancellor.
Beneficiaries of their foresight and generosity—
the pioneers who placed our haven here
where life takes place—where love's incipient,
for each one circling the observatory.
It hurts so bad to never speak with you.

II

HOMAGE TO WELDON KEES

The variegated coastlines of disjunctive
blue grey technicolor roofs and rain
surmise the cat's walk. Coming on the plane
the thick bouquet of lights was sparkling thicker
than all of twenty years before. You wrote—
I was not there to answer. I was not there.

It is the most I can do to recall
what I'm not even sure was ever real—
gardens that were built before we were born
that seemed to draw us into a lost time,
invitations that were archetypal.
Under than rain it's as if life begins,
and is a thing we never knew before …
so wonderful the night must die with it.

III

Starting from Top of Vallejo, Second Night

Then out of the darkness as if with no past
shadow itself turned to shadow not there.
They say the killer walks here every day.
The body hangs where flowers do not care
in the thick thicket turning the same way.
The killer is not reproached; he *is* reproached.
Who would want to litter in San Francisco?
You could get infected, you could die.
I've never heard such silence in my life,
silence of knowing no one and the wind,
the absolute silence of a noisy wind.
Then there are the chimes, they chime ten years
or more. The pearls go over the bridge,
far more worse than being misunderstood.
This is right. This is comeuppance. Reality.

Don't you ever wonder what we missed?
There is a private lookout which was built
behind Coit Tower, an inverted gorge,
thin wood-railed precipice the cat defends.
To hell with how most people are—the roofs
are something else again, a life unlived.
A summer magnified to many years.
This tier of gardens like the heart of man,
maze-like as all appendages of time,
the secret chambers stacked to tantalize,
long passages that open in the brush.

Admit it's sad to know that you will die.
Not only they did, meaning of *before,*
but disappeared into another day
of hallowed plantings and of hallowed stone.

Smell of remembrance! Birds of Florida!
Too much of tourist's tan new leather. Prop
of regeneration. Glen plaid and white slacks.
It hardly makes a difference, but what does
is scattered among the pigeons and the gulls
and the wide gravel of the pier's warehouse,
the tattooed sparkle of the denizens.
See you at Costo. I am parting thus.
One feels so much freer in California.

DIVINE RIGHTS

The marriage of druids and Romans
write it
I don't even know how to spell it
It is my real birth today Cadwaladr

Why would they marry?
Where is everything
I am the descendent
        of the king
They were protecting
        the son of
            the king
not father
mother

Landis
Mary
The Poet King
I knew all this
I know all this
We must have been
at alliance with the Scottish.
We must have
been at war
with the Irish
        king.
I know these things.
Freud got it right.
But it is a
throwing off

of kings.
The English King.
The English Queen.
And what am I to think of the English queen,
    Elizabeth?
Or the Russian? Familiar as the lion.
Landis, descended from Charlemagne
and twin Dutch admirals?
Or the Scottish princess in the west?

The prophecy told
    me too
    it is true
after I was thirty-five
    I would be king
would regain my
    forgotten kingdom
what this means
    would be revealed
    would be recovered
every time I had my
        hand read
    or my cards told
Now it has come
    on my real day
        of birth

Florence
after Troy
in the confining hour of our winter

How would you be able to know
you were able to be the mother
of the father
of the king?

often assisted by the Scottish

Herb Hillman
Karen Penn
The Holy Experiment
The Sword in the Stone.
Arthur.
Murphy the Irish King?

The is the subject of my poetry.
The Prodigal
The Return
Eliot is sympathetic
What is he to me?
An English prince
and friend of the Welsh King?
Prince Charles
is not the true prince
Was there a son?
Was he the son of Baumgarten?
So then who is Sylvia?
Get out of my castle.
I must go to Wales.
The Faerie Queene is probably

a political commentary on
the lineage of the kings.

When I was five years old
my father
the ward of the king
took me to see
the sword of the lake
splitting the mountain
in an old storm.
la la

They told me
    when I was a child
but I didn't listen
    That's what my
poetry is about
    warmest verse

Musing upon the king my brother's wreck
All I want to know about are kings

These source materials which have lasted longest,
elements of narrative which have stayed the same
longest. Those which have proved most popular.

The Beginning
The Return
The Kitchen
Winter

The insult given Branwen by the Irish
At Guinnion Fort
Arthur bore the image of Mary as his sign
Arcturus or the keeper of the Pole
and thus it was I watched the turn of winter

'I have made a heap of all that i could find' Nennius
        (Historia Brittonum).
an 'inward wound'
caused by the fear that certain things dear to him should be
        'like smoke dissipated' (Jones/Nennius, 1951)
i'm guessing in the old cosmology it wd be the first 24 hrs of
        your actual presence
and i'll attribute that to bertrand russell. these are just
        notes.—don marquis (1922)

romeo & juliet in berkeley
i was surprised he looked so much like me
disguise him not to look like myself
i remember
he the leviathan in all ages
my father one eyed introduced me to him

(the currence of the past holds own
our against the recogsentiment
or winds like the runner on the shore
away from the sun in a steady
exhalation, at a vast limit of the net
where one exists in a continuum

spreading in a few words
a striding reach up morning—

he's there in all his incarnations)

a date engraved in bronze swings in its chains
under moon under midnight in its bondless bonds
citizenless entropy of stars, what is heard
never viewd as it is, which is as it is not.
Is never as it can be understood,
must by definition answer nothing.
There is no fixing of these loci.

Iwerddon
And they began the banquet and caroused and discoursed.
And when it was more pleasing to them to sleep than to
        carouse,
they went to rest, and that night Branwen came
Matholwch's bride.
101 Dalmations

Look in the mirror and you will recall
the white snow of an earlier snow-fall,
how dragon behind rock had threatened rook,
and rains had formed the letters of a book
in which our love is written. Dragon, look.
How queer. The snows of yesteryear are here.

His mother was the daughter of the king
his son her brother and his uncle

who from earliest winter in the kitchen
stood stirring, sifting, towering
in the first curl of the bird's branch
close to him then she made his song
too-wit too-wit tu-lily hi-li-ly tu-wit tu-lo
and interbranched and interladen among the
hyacinth, jack o'whirl o' shadow—
cleaving densities of variant dispersals,
gravities which undercut propensity:
proofs of an undisclosed philately.
Mad's progress relays Delft into land smile
under the textile's firm approval—
Barkowitz', Horovitz' room. Seal approval.
A real anger at dates. Back in dense sandal word—
I see trees, people dancing in the trees,
a formal approval of glass on paper.
Mixing spices like nutmeg and cinnamon.
Looking up the stovepipe for listening last years.
Another one, only as she could have been.

All around us, the snow in the forest.
Snow walking up hill in the forest,
through snow walking up hill.
I was born in the forest.
I was born under the snow.
I would rather be snowed under
than to have to go in to dinner.
I would rather be lost, out of all ear.
Where the ice thunder with its own snow choir.

Where repetitive naming is lost on hard vortex.
Edge

Their darkness is the sleep in her eyes,
before parting.

Tu-wit. And cherry.
Twice cherry. Cherry Street, and cheery
cheery cherry in the song, all along.
A name for marble torsos and a night port,
everything you wrote in the guest book.
A quick way to do the invitations in summer.
The inn I am staying in, and what a bother.
Why you never answered embroidered on the hem of your
sweater.

We were in the mountains. This genius
was in trust to the genius of the forest.
She didn't nothing that she didn't do.
The forest was a game, where I was first
the others were blind, even she my mother
which meant that I was king.
I have seen these things before they happen.
I have seen her bake day into evening,
have seen her bake the forest into evening,
have seen her bake the hour of homecoming.
The birds are details in her narrative,
ingredients recipes get around to having.
Talk is sure word made out of it,
I wouldn't in wind or rain doubt it,

to gather or collect to retell or rerecollect
every word which the father
brought home for him to inspect.

Why then a king
through kinship of a lady?
A virgin birth. Her mother was king,
I do not doubt it,
upon the plains that have no need of naming.
Why then a king took consecrated ground
which was to plainer eye unconsecrated.
Poetry appears to be living.
I heard it strike the sky like keel and thunder
worn into evening like a headline's banter.
I saw it grab my hand like dad in winter.
I walked it home, the sky ripped at the center,
dark merchant hulk. Perpetual, aimless
Leviathan which strikes the heart of time.
My first knowledge of a light in winter.

And when I first returned to town,
nothing shook my memory,
I never saw
the fiery medal
in my own hand,
dull like my days.
Often quoted
early in spring.

Or noticed how my aunt cast
familiar stories against a local past.

The mystery of the virgin mother
it self would appear to have to reappear.
No wonder I didn't get any idea
nor wonder if you too don't get an idea
why none of this was going to simply appear.

I saw this in the absolute symmetry of the outlines
of the bathtub in the apartment in the city in the world
in our time and in all time

The still being there of the resurrection

Time which comes
only to those it visits.

Why then a birth of kings among the females?

And wasn't a female the king of the king?

*　　*　　*

I've reached territory.

And so I have been protected from marriage.
So too the quelling of the Jewish King.

For Christ must be his Jew
and virgin birth.

I scarcely thought I could return to her.
But remember how I saw myself
under her influence, her double image
binding the speech of then
with speech to come.

The gods are merchants at these dinners.
Maecenas never dilutes his pleasure.

I didn't think they were
serious. But the king was her
and industry among the settlers
lingers without artifact.

You could say she was worth waiting for.
To have seen her
with nothing to spoil the mood
properly in winter.

What made her special
was what she would become.
This was the meaning of the pristine forest
in which you could see the verb repeating,
always showing in numeric mimicry
the voice in the breath
the eye in the imagery

a deep syntax
of auditory visuality:
for that heard of voices
implies the wind has been
where you yourself have.

The newness of those days,
when these were first.

Mixing the silk and sand of salt and sugar
into the flour. Vanilla in the spoon
darkly reflecting her double down the hallway
and upside down up under her apron.
The fortress of butter malleable to time,
beating the retreating oil slick
in the flood of mud.
A sea of milk.

They brought me many designs of Venice silk.
I paid them to stand around, because I was cold.
I wanted to know what they aspired to.
I am his wreck, and him his father's before me.
I like the charge of shadow without name.

And as we watched enacted in the play
he say to her what I to you would say
and she to he what you would say to me,
so we both watch to see how things will end.
You but remember to be a friend.
You greet me unannounced. I come in rain.

And only this remains to be said,
I have come to rid the land of Saxons.

*   *   *

Rehearsals of the shadows where you stood
before you have returned into the halls.

And why no mother of a Jewish King
if not a Jewish King within the line?

One Bad King

Then in my grief
I ran into the wood
along the lake's edge,
out of ear shot.
And as I sped
into a gallop
covering much ground,
passing many trees,
not many thoughts
separated from my friends,
who found the tree
of inner light
in which the Welsh King
put his head
before he knew
he was the King,

I saw I was transformed
into a flying horse
and coiled myself
within the forest's nest
to dully sleep
to hear the distant
fall of words
turn into footsteps
of my friends,
covering the woods.
So I would have the apples speak to me.
So I would have this orchard speak to me.

If my blood
could get back in touch with you.
Shannon
Welsh girl with an Irish name.
I am missing from these documents.

Fifty years
after the war
I saw the dead
returning home
on _____ Way.

Then
I was at his house
which was the house
I came from
when I was his

father who I greet.
Under
a rain
the blue city
has the same look
that her eyes had
in her round head
the Scottish Queen.

In that hour
when memory settles
on the evening
darkness its liquid
history of masks,
I quote you
and see the world
as written on the dark sky.
They rearrange
as flame
and fly to conspire
with my father
who is leading us
under the mountain
to the sea beast.
Always outside the room
               in which we talk
above us
         where what must be the roof
is how I see it
if we don't lie and confer,

a mixing of night and day
in which the heart's first urge
speaks, but in words of fire.
They know the night
who came here first
and them I see
in my words' end.

Even then
I knew these things could be without me.
But that I was the King
I saw unknowing.
The first song of spring
in my upbringing.
A curator of lies.
A curator of sleep.
Shut up with your eyes.
I am the King
and I have broken darkness.

Look in the storm.
Look in the barrel.
Look under the mountain.
I am the dragon.

Look where her room
retains the look
of the room of a stranger,
now in the east. Where we began.

I named you then
the Hyacinth girl.
Words that were meant for no other,
as has long been known in the land.

Separating at night.
Ten years in arms.
Talked of as if it happened yesterday.
Cried the ladies,
the vegetables that name themselves.

Mother then
I am your son
the King.

EPILOGUE

It is youth that understands old age
and your repulsion is but a projection
an image of the loathing you obtain.
I've seen the fall come in and think I shall
follow each leaf that winds about the house
to where you stutter, the end of the tether
where grace walks through the bridal foliage
and no one could mistake you for another.
After that, they are only leaves to burn.
And when the flowers burst upon the rain
the roofs shall keep their solemn gentle witness
far from the young men who travel far
to fill their noses with the autumn air.
Daybreak is decent as awakening.
And love is gentle, though he is no scholar.
What if I filled my notebook with his words
sketched suddenly with no least hesitation
would she return to him when it came fall
or would she sink into a bitter winter
not even counting the blossoms that are gone.
How many times the autumn rain recurs
to wind about the river in the evening
or fall like one great ocean in the dawn.
No matter, he has had enough of her
and leaves his youth in hope of something better.
A drop expresses all the flooding water,
the wind instills the trees with sentiment,
and no one, no one can reverse the patter
of the darkness that's enclosed within.

It stares across the city in the dawn
and cannot wake these shrouds of memory.

JANUARY 2008 (2010)

Frankenstein the aviator flew
eleven feet indoors. No one ever knew.
He had perfected the bearings of steel
and got his airplane off the ground by feel.
He liked his poetry, and he liked Vienna,
and he liked a simple girl called Hannah.
She would mend his socks and cook his stew
while silently his mathematics grew.
All this took place before 1911
and was not published till 1927.
Those who knew him, who were very few
wondered at his strength of solitude.
He himself had written an etude
to celebrate the secrets of the nude.
Some of his students thought he might be gay.
But every winter he went away
to Austria and never said a word.
Life to him was something he had heard.

In Mrs. Gardener's boudoir
we smoked hashish and drank champagne
on Christmas eve. Below, the choir
of off-guard duties rendered pain
among the Singers, while we played
a Chopin prelude, improvised,
manic, on Paderewski's frayed
piano, which was ill-advised.

NEW POEMS (2013)

Dinner Conversation

Dinner conversation. A blank slate
on which to install the empire. Josephus dreams
of decorating silk screens with battle scenes.
Arminius and Varus. Hilda and Hildegaard
turn slightly green but take it not that hard
when Harry with jet-streaked curls of Roman silver
flicks thick ashes into a samovar.
Piles of ripe fruit. How many poppy seeds
will we require to satisfy our needs.
Archie and Jughead analyse the field.
All is statistics, with a fudge sundae sealed.
Silence and talk are two different kinds of power.
"I have to work." The ruling class
wishes to suffer. The poor sit on their ass.
History and archaeology revive
fear of the gods, the instinct to take a wife.
A rich man's daughters are posted to inventories.
The visiting statesman approves of the lawn frieze.
The Botticelli bursts another spring.
It is of florentine silks that I shall sing.
This rough and tumble clan
will expire in madness to a man.
Ah, to be truly mad, that must be glorious,
to see each word as a sign and write in prose.
Lisa puts my toy football in her bra,
and then lifts up her shirt for me to see,
pink white breasts in magnolia taffeta.
My one wish, that I shall soon go blind!
To stop these visions dancing in my mind.
In my dream they thought I had stolen clothes

(books I had borrowed from the library).
The horizon is never permitted to doze.
The real shipment of gold
is emblazoned in flames for all to see.

POEM FOR THE FIRST DAY OF SPRING

The vampire's coffin in Los Angeles
is kept company by an ape named Barabas.
Sunlight through the basement windows all day
projects dust motes where the ape and the coffin play.
This shadow was once a movie star, this grave
is a science experiment that the last actors crave.
Whoever comes here, Thelma or Clara or Theda,
will go in silence, paying homage to Rita.
Children come home from school, but that is all.
The lawn is trimmed, and the slate arches pall.

Avion, Gorrion

Avion, Gorrion.
What does this mean?
DC-3 divisible by three.
A bilingual entelechy.
When it was raining
a man stopped into the store,
emerging from the street
as the street must have been
to him, entering the store.
He asked for a book that didn't exist,
but were his questions answers
that didn't exist, but for me.
The rain grew darker, and the quiet louder,
separate from what we were here for,
veering into ideas of evenings just around the corner
like streaks of newsprint honouring the living,
promising a glitter of excited chatter
and the audible crackle of a firm reply
in a dry room where a fresh gaze amplifies
the removal of a jacket to an unlooking chair,
where a cloud shifts in the glint of an eye,
glowing and growing on embroidery flowering,
sinking into a gutter of loneliness
where everything that happens is obscured,
where darkness and silence become comforting
because familiar, locking the library
while other people rush to see a play.
Cocktails and cigarettes, warmer, more rapidly
affirm the towering city,
and yet apart from it I saw you were

in need of identifying in thin layers
in circles turning, what you were
as if some smile were rained on high above
the revelers distracted from their hearing,
looked on and looking on
in the frank moment of your naked gaze,
as if you put it in a question to me,
that I hesitating not to answer
revealed like thunder in rained on eyes.
A sudden meaning of the printed flower.

And what of
avion, Gorrion.
A bilingual entelechy.
What do the letters dispense with,
do they recall
forms or patterns of a habit
knowing for an unknown name.
I put it to you.
Do these omissions
exceed their tolerance
for identity ungroping to be blind.
Reaching like a bomb or gun
into the alert heart.
Most of history is lost.
These stories (rain-like chatter) point away from
jade and onyx halls the mind caresses
caught like a mirror in its desperation.
Fantastic corridors eight arms of Buddha
retain the silence of a sentence on.

Corridors that lead to many rooms
where nothing is known, or what is known,
enacted before, conspires discreetly
to initiate salvation
in evil, heaping plunder of trade,
glittering treasure so fabulous
it cannot be measured except in legend.
Removed rooms, if they exist.
Where yet upon the eve of some great journey
travelers share a meal in conversation
only dimly aware of being watched,
of activities their splendid host conceals,
unthreatening, unknowable,
the unknowing that pleasure itself delights in,
tasting rare delicacies of an exotic host.
Behind the surface what was never asked,
something to lose in pondering over sleep,
with the next day looking like lace over high cut glass,
in the image of a man inside a man,
impossible doubt left hanging, or erased.

And what of
avion, Gorrion.
Is there somewhere another,
architect, painter,
proficient in the classical arts,
to be forgotten, as if the age uproots
its mirror image, recalls strict languages
of the hour after dinner,
the unknowable brother.

The dents insert a slight influence
on schemes of color, on whole forms of classical music
kept in the silence of a marble sculpture,
opened only in the thin hours
before others wake.
Agreed upon
as if an entertainment
could ally the feelings
of what each keeps
in a back drawer, with scissors and paste and tape.
This is not that other
finding himself
seized in the midst
of a dying city
where all voices blur
bright in blindness,
the brushstroked paint
of an absolute color
in a small town's wake.
A clown seized in madness,
admitting and exonerating nothing.

Avion. Gorrion.
Say it again, but do not understand
the imprint of its meaning.
Cease to leave its foul importance
settling in a corner, in obscurity.
There is no need to understand or visit
what has been left behind, what cannot name itself

for fear of belying its greater importance,
stumbled on, perhaps, in the rain.

CIRQUE D'ETOILES

And after all is made a frozen waste
of snow and ice, of boards and rags ...
if I should see one spark of permanent,
one chink of blue among the wind-blown slags
approaching thus, and mirroring my surmise,
one liquid frozen permanence, your eyes ...
should meet you at the end of time
and never end ...
for always, even past death, you are my friend ...
and when at last it comes, inevitable,
that you shall sit in furs at high table
(for what other fate can one expect?)
dispensing honours, correlating plans
for every cause, for education, science ...
what will I miss? how can I not be there?
who see you sputtering wordless in despair ...
as I do now "miss nothing, nothing"
and to know you are some other man's
(the stupid jerk), who once had your compliance ...
and do these things ever end? (and if so, where?)
I ask myself, and should I feel despair?
to know, to love, to know, and still not care?
in winter, spring, and summer, and in fall,
on land or sea, at any time at all,
to know that half the stars on each night shine,
the other half are in your eyes, and mine ...
and what is there? And what, I ask, is there?
Only these hurt and wounded orbs I see
nestled against a frozen stark brick wall ...
and there are you, and there is me,

and that is all, that is all …
How from this torment can I wrestle free?
I can't … for thus is my soliloquy.
And you shall sit there serving backers tea.
And running ladies circles. Think of me …
Think of me, when like a mountainous waste
the night's long dreaming stretches to a farther coast
where nothing is familiar … two paths that may have
        crossed
discover what had long been past recall …
that nothing's really changed at all,
that we are here!
Here among flowering lanterns of the sea,
finite, marking each vestige of the city
with trailing steps, with wonder, and with pity!
And laugh, and never say that you feel shitty,
are one whose heart is broken, like this ditty.
And think that there is nothing there to miss.
Think "I must not miss a thing. I must not miss
the wraps, the furs, the teaspoon, or the kiss."
And end in wishes. And leave not this abyss.
For all is one, beginning as it's done.
Never forgetting this, till I am no one.
There is no formula that can forget …
these eyes pierce though ten thousand suns have set,
and will keep setting … now tuck in your head,
the blankets folded, and lay down in your bed.
And stir the stars, long after we are dead.

SONNETS FROM *THE KING*

I

How often their predictable voices jostling the night air
within a scent's reach of jonquils and jasmine
and the eyes' blinded reach of the insoluable sphinx
turn ideas in themselves—a circulating zephyr—
too loudly, paradaisal and prismatic:
the silver words!—Death's stealth
relinquishes finally nothing but their motion;
British, French, Turkish, German, Arabic,
mean nothing to the eclipsing god,
their silence wrought in menacing origin,
that has no halve, killing them where they're standing.
The useless breasts, diminutive exchanges,
live in the shadow of their apocalyptic
certainty: beyond which there is nothing.

Why do the lovers speak
if not to disturb and unsettle eternal darkness?

XXVI

These laundry lines lead nowhere, whipped by rain.
Perhaps each in some window survives a stain.
Impenetrable cubicles, stacked and spread out grid
fortified and multiplied by discolored brick
and blocks of concrete emptied of their makers.
The sky drifts black and blue, but no one sees
primordial origins, stark auguric trees,
pretexts of order crumbling to disorder.
Death shakes the silence that the worn heart leaves.

XXXVI

for Isabel Biderman

Finally to see with eyes of onyx and jade—
what's always there. Cleopatra with her crown
gives O's for X's, gives X's for O's
perpetually working towards the city's center
by katty-corner, wishes too grand to grant
—for who can both live in the rarest palace
and be its guest? Passing again and again
brings nothing closer—a few feet in the end
and all is different. Different and the same!
A better life, taller and rising to heaven
(the dog escapes, returns according to plan).
Fabulous laughter lives in the hereafter.
The cat withdraws into its impregnable dream.
The actor leaving the palace is just a man.

XXXVII

Each is the same, each different and the same.
The most fabulous windows let three sets of eyes
aligned at Christmas, at the center of the world,
admire its fusion of the past and future,
one after another, converting pleasure from pain,
in endless profusion, each image containing each image,
imponderably long, too long for the eyes to sustain
for its duration: faith and hope and renewal!
The makers of the world gather each jewel
with humour and innovation
and admiration of the classic forms
defying dispersion: and glittering with grace!
Mapping with silver and pearls the planets in space!
Each, one by one, her pilgrimage to that place.

XXXVIII

The motors roar! No calendars erase
each different corner that they signify,
though each is drenched in darkness! And perfumes,
like vintage draughts and plumage that caress
the mind's thumbprint-tip, periscope windowscapes
elapsing into silence, gone too fast.
Where they remain—as if ever they stood
imagination to its single undrinkable clasp
in primitive tribal echoes no word can grasp
except as a hieroglyph—untested, real,—
are only verified in what we feel
we know, so staggeringly slow
they speed up till they are backwards before they go,
in pillowed images, stung by the asp.

XXXX

In the garden the night is directionless,
the wind one wind, unfathomably far
and relinquishing time in its shrill precipice.
The flowers stand and shine, returning no images.
From what corner have they come,
standing sentry apart from all the sleepers,
as if one permanent incognizable sign
to be read in the cosmos for an eternity.
The basement casements, dusty with disuse,
convey with their impregnably abstruse
recalcitrance an inner life, to all
who are among the living of no use.
The wide walkways of the stars divide
chapters of our lives like music in reverse.

XXXXI

These inner courtyards frame at least as well
the towering cognizances like a sea of soup
that hem in all that you can never tell.
The bricks besplatter clatter, drown and droop
in the time's eye that waits too long for you
who betoken all that you have to do
and still surmise the patchwork of the skies
that spanks all basketballs and infancies
where the brick prisons rise and the trees trough
the fog as if it couldn't get enough
of being, and where you look as of surprise!
Retired on night busses these secrets doff
their caps, and settling their feet up
look westward upon each immaculate roof
as if it might be home. Drink from this cup.

Ben Mazer

ENTERING THE CITY OF NEW YORK

Entering the city of New York,
is something like approaching ancient Rome,
to see the living people crawling forth,
each pipe and wire, window, brick, and home.

The times are sagging, and it is unreal
to know one's slice of mortal transient time.
We angle forward, stunned by what we feel,
like insects, incognizant of every crime.

We are so duped, who make up civilization
in images of emotions that we feel,
to know the ague of the mortal steel,
each one perched balanced at his separate station.

The graves are many, and their fields decay,
where nothing can be meant to stand forever.
No doubt in due course God will have his way,
and slowly, slowly, all our bonds dissever.

But we shall not be here to see it happen;
we will have left this world behind to others;
there is no silent power who is mapping
our hearts and wishes, or those of our brothers.

Lift high the head, and let the jaunty scarf
blow in the reckless wind of each new morning;
walk to the edge of each old well-used wharf
and see imprinted there time's towering warning.

See with fresh eyes the little that we are,
the stump, the shattered window, and time's scar;
beating your chest, exult to have come so far;
stand at the edge of time's still promontory,
accepting your role in the unwritten story,
where lethe-wards we travel in the dory
of each borrowed, rented, dented car.

The lives are many, and the riches few,
though somewhere they are fabulously piled,
as useless to the living man as to
forgotten kings through whose fingers they have filed.

Particulars of prowess, social standing,
all equally must face God's reprimanding,
until all stretches out in endless sands,
and each no longer knows his lover's hands.

The cantors and the funerals have plied
their rituals in small communities,
each like the many others that precede it,
poor orphans of the storm, we must concede it.

Delicatessens all are richly piled
with meats and cheeses, treasures, delicacies;
each generation goes, but all are styled
upon the blueprints of established keys.

Impoverished lovers huddled in the doorways,
of ancient carvings and dishonoured brick,

all have their fabled, tragically real stories,
exalted till time exerts its famous prick.

The painted lover in his walled-in room
must pace and fret, exerting to be known
the meagre wishes that he calls his own,
in sparkling breakfasts that relieve his gloom.

Stand on the kingly carvings of a coin,
and looking down, see where each crevice lies,
aloft the damp pianos, each mouldy groin
of wall and carpet's strict amenities.

And when the night takes cover, letting in
a maelstrom of resurgences, begin
to lengthen prospects of a shadow ghost
of gestures, particulars where you have been!

An alley narrows to a drop of rain
that knows no patron but the valent skin
of shoe-wet footsteps, brave beyond all pain;
without a name then, let your life begin.

With Caligari at Octoberfest,
and on into the night, where wind-spires send
unopened messages to scattered streets
toward which our passions shall unfettered bend!

These spectral certainties have no clear end,
although they are not mapped, but constancies

of one ghost city, upon which we attend,
exult to hold us steady, mobile in their seas!

And into ladies parlours, balls defunct,
the presence hounds the night and jars the shutters,
exempting no absence or childhood spent half-bunked,
seeking that other who at the top opera stair utters!

For there, for there, at the top opera stair ...
one perfect innocence exuding stars
that join the heavens, violet and dense,
lies at the heart of love that truly matters!

In an unopened box, these presents rest,
meant for some other fortune has more blessed;
for now, let all desire overcome
with sleep, nurture, solidify love's kingdom!

In zig zag byways of the shopworn heart,
each one extends his own ghost-flooded streams,
makes tribute to traditions he will own
until the many faces all must marry
impalpably the universal mart,
to be reborn in some late other's dreams!

A Dream

I was the last to understand
what she had never understood.
How Washington and Talleyrand
had made her sad to make her good.
From Nashville to the Cumberland
her father owned five hundred slaves
who grew tobacco on the land.
God bless the innocence of knaves.
I met her on a dark strange night
in Clarksville, in a gothic manse.
And knew that nothing had been right,
for too much had been left to chance.
The child was hers, and not some man's.
She fled New Jersey, went back home.
She turned down every plea to dance,
until her tears began to come.
And talked of how they had to bury
dark secrets of the cemetery.
How on the graves young men made merry
until she had been forced to marry.
How in the morning she reviled
herself, and felt most sick.
How after the divorce was filed
no other man could do the trick.
Until she met a gentle sort,
who did not know a woman's heart.
How she consented to his court,
and made with him an honest start.
How half her daughter's mind was black
with demons, and a father's lack.

Why did she tell these things to me,
most gracious on a dark strange night
beneath a wilted, haunted tree,
in terrible, distorted light,
as if these truths were half my right?
I'll never see her kind again,
most captive in her yellow gown.
Her beauty reached from now to then.
Her smile has left me with a frown.

GOLDEN BOY

Up there where decision drives like an implacable wind
the division between what is desired and what is demand,
the top of the city seems suddenly explicable
and reality itself the foremost fable,
whether rich or poor, whether in or out the door.
The hand freezes brushing against hair, brushing against
       another,
whether a small daughter growing to be a wife and a mother,
and the insistence to fall is tearfully bitter,
to fail to succeed seems to be elaborately better.
But to convince her, who holds the key to it all,
with the double doorway of her half-cowed allegiances,
is equal to an entire lifetime of stress,
broken hands, the spurned violin, the old world father's
       distress,
the decision to ride by a cab to the upper side,
the stark silvery icy refusal to take a dive.
For now is now, and nothing anyone can say,
can never again take the smallest of dreams away,
whether they let him go, chalking him up as crazy,
or do him bad, stating that he is lazy.
No matter, here, now, at the top of the world,
in the massive city, undulating and whirled
on the silver spikes of hope, the beams of lights
that crush the weak, debilitate their spirits,
like shadows he sees the spirits of all his fights
fall away, knowing love in a grain of sand, in one of the
       world's nights.

Monsieur Barbary Brecht

Who shall it fall upon to inspect
the comings and goings of Anthony Hecht?
The Cummings and Boeings, the strummings and knowings,
the summings and flowings of Anthony Hecht?

Maybe the Master, the shepherd and pastor,
the leopard, lean, faster,
that peppered forecaster,
the Phoenix and Castor, Monsieur Barbary Brecht!

Who will exhume the intelligent wanderings,
the diplomat, coup de tat, government squanderings,
and furious ponderings also that stem thereof,
and fonder things, of the late Howard Nemerov?

No one more furious, curious, serious,
sometimes delerious, always imperious,
mighty ambiguous, slightly conspicuous,
Jane Geoffrey Simpleton—Monsieur Barbary Brecht!

Who will expose as verbose the rich prose,
will deface and erase its slick surface with grace,
will unweave what he wove, and enclose what there flows,
of the flaws of the prose of Ernest Fellose?

No one more hounding, more pounding, more counting,
more hunting, or cunting, or brushed up with bunting,
than that master of everything Asians depict,
and the roots of all madness—Monsieur Barbary Brecht!

Actually what is it, I'm trying to say,
tomorrow, tonight, yesterday and today,
intangible, frangible, Monsieur John Mandeville,
irreversible, curseable, not nearly nurseable,
something appealing to Barbara Hutton,
I'm trying to turn myself off, but I can't find the button.
I tell myself, you should be more circumspect,
for one who's the houseguest of Monsieur Barbary Brecht!

General Walker inspired a stalker,
who hired John Pauker to be a big talker,
in Dallas with Alice, with much forethought malice,
his background they checked and they checked and they
        checked.

And though it was hot, and he took a pot shot,
played his part to the hilt, revealed nothing of guilt,
even when questioned by George Mohrenschildt,
who had made him defect?—Monsieur Barbary Brecht!

There are two different kinds of fuck.
The fuck that's fucked, and the fuck that's fucked.
And in Algeria—last time I checked—
both were reserved for Monsieur Barbary Brecht!

Professor Pitkins had a real tight jaw.
Perhaps he even wore a metal bra.
But if he did the one who could detect
that this was so was Monsieur Barbary Brecht!

If you see W.H. Auden you might just have boughten
a diversion, a version, a red and dread sturgeon,
a false bill of goods, and you may have been tricked
by that master of everything which has been bricked,
the one they call mother—Monsieur Barbary Brecht!

But apart from this world, where the great winds are whirled,
and the towers are darkened, childs play
with primordial knowing of Hindoos and fairies
and Edmund St. Bury's, and all that's most out of the way—
they may dig holes to China, or reveal their vagina
(in the hall suits of armour compelling good karma)
but no matter how darkness betray
the extent of the world, or the word, they have trekked
through inversions of Monsieur Barbary Brecht!

The ghost in the wainscot is trembling and bludgeoned
and wrapped in a fox that is dry and curmudgeoned
but the thespian sheets fly aloft in the air
and although there is tea, there is nobody there.

There is no one to draw lines with pen and with ink,
or to stain with hair coloring half of the sink,
but the wrought iron is animated, and the architect
of this elaborate absence is Monsieur Barbary Brecht!

Try typing his name and you might go insane,
at the way the hands work towards each other and then
go in circles repeating again and again
one insistent motif like a tom-tom refrain,

and then spiral upwards—an enigma machine
couldn't do it the justice of how it is whacked
on a simple corona—Monsieur Barbary Brecht!

In the hall the rich children glare and they stare
at the poor little visitor who enters there,
his musical prodigy greater than theirs
sends them scuttling in snide little groups up the stairs.
But the hostess is compassionate and hands him a score,
but he just doesn't feel up to play any more,
and wonders what lies behind the magnificent door
where the children all vanished, and his vision is flecked
by the shadowy mustache of Monsieur Barbary Brecht!

If I were a 1926 model Ford
I would carry your body and then I'd have poured
it over the bridge and into the river
without so much as the least tiny shiver.—
So the love letters of little girls run
but they never have ever so nearly much fun
as the brain that delights behind eyes that reflect
the abductions of Monsieur Barbary Brecht!

It is Christmas time and the world is still
and the windows like lenses of glass that are cracked
where the presents are stacked on the shelves do not kill
the spirit of our saviour who's come from afar
for whom the child left the door slightly ajar
the deciduous rustle of Hyperborean pines
shuffles in the three wise men and the brilliant star shines

and no one, but no one could ever detect
the immaculate presence of Monsieur Barbary Brecht!

The spires of Mem Hall, and what's trapped in the cat,
like the great North wind go this way and that,
and no matter how anyone's ever detained
by a shivery feeling, a vague sense of what's stained
by what came before us, or what's not yet come,
there isn't a formula for doing the sum,
yet all of your queries you might kindly direct
to the highly compassionate Monsieur Barbary Brecht!

The fire's last flicker as it falls in the shadows
leaves all in the darkness of its afterglows.
The winter winds whistle, and somewhere a thistle
is lodged in a crevice of snows.
Mother and father, sister and brother,
the family's together, and all will protect
the spirit of Christmas, and sing the great missal,
in the translation of Monsieur Barbary Brecht!

Behind every brick there's a visual trick,
an encapturement that's luminoso,
in the rain, in the brain, in the strain, in the wane
of enrapturement, tres furioso.
It's a kind of a click, that may not or may stick,
and may trap what I meant, I suppose so.
Like back issues of old magazines might reflect
a spectrum of tissues—Monsieur Barbary Brecht!

Dante and Berryman, and Bernard Herriman!
All can be found here, can be seen in sound here!
It makes no difference what order, what corridor,
except as causation's perceived as sensation,
no border can thwart or export or condense here
or give any quarter to the immense sense here
of Nemerov, Tamiroff, Bellow or Hecht—
all one, the domain of Monsieur Barbary Brecht!

So tell me, just how if they are indivisible
we need them. We seed them when they are invisible!
The order they cede to is perfectly cracked.
Call in the correctives—Monsieur Barbary Brecht!

The films of the forties, the great women's films,
are baked on the surfaces of post boxes and kilns,
like the whisper of porcelain, the threads of empire,
that visit the sky and retire in a spire,
they expire in the senses, for one and for all,
one vast waiting ocean, the windows recall,
with curtains and windowseats holding hopes checked,
but nothing's arrived today—Monsieur Barbary Brecht!

The Alps

Yet here, in these Alps,
where each one is a stranger,
where no one senses danger,
there is no need to hold a door
with a vacant eye, disturbing the mountains.
The floorboards clog, but will be dry
when the spring comes. Or is it spring?
Each one turns the latch, and lets it swing,
each in his sweater makes the floor grow wetter,
each thinks that he is better.
And the math problems go unsolved.
Yet each one is resolved,
with his senses closed, his face close to the paper,
and the pen scurrying, the heart burying
the look of each stranger, through the door hurrying,
resolved to solving problems with no end,
let no man say that this one is his friend.
When the spring comes
the Colombian Greek or Russian Spaniard
gesticulates wildly, blocking the cafe floor,
and the black countess is in love with him no more.
What has she to lose?
She titters wildly like a goose
and though her eyes pop wide
she doesn't see the man in mocha brown
who stands in the door, looks up and then looks down.
And why should she complain?
She, who has been numb too long for pain,
who doesn't notice there is any strain.
And no one here has cabin fever!

The most lost one is like an eager beaver,
asking to be called Tiresias.
Even through restraint they make a fuss,
saying—you are one of us.
But I, I drink my coffee and scan my paper,
alone I see the man in mocha brown,
and though I have no sense of any caper,
I watch his eyes look down,
and wait for the entire afternoon to taper.

At the Tabuki Kabuki

She was a hothouse flower, but she grew
to such proportions that she never knew
her brand of people, less her brand of steeple,
and saw things as they happened, from the view.

Her husband took her on his trips to Asia,
to count the factories, and meet the heads
of government and business. In her beds
were flowers, chocolates, cinctures of aphasia.

In time the path sloped upward, and the driver
relaxed a bit, began to tell his story.
It grew less clear just who was driving who,
she, the loquacious one, or he, the taciturn McGiver,

or if it was a modern sort of dory.
As she listened, she began to rue
the little fables, and the many tables,
and the entire vast illusion, too.

New South Wales

Splendid the glorious technicolor gales
that break the unbreakable spirit in New South Wales.
All tends towards dawn, but night is strange and long,
plays out a drama where there's something wrong
that's never said. The green balustrades
are freely entered by too well trusted maids.
The carelessly worn inscription at the approach
to the manor is a mildly forbidding reproach.
The table's set for six deceptive men
who drink together and remember when
they all were younger, fates were sealed in anger.
The shabby port which doubles as a border
tries to preserve some semblance of royal order.
The governor bathes, is briefed on each new stranger
holding some parcel of land with his fierce will.
True friendship survives the time it learned to kill.
The sobbing of the old life's worn bud quails.
A chrysalis is born in New South Wales.

Hell's Angels

Three Oxford chums, but one of them was German,
before the war, with April blossoming
and the bright futures, subject to the king.
Now paired to death, uncompromising quota,
defensively aggressive last iota,
he swooned and realized he was his sister,
fired one last shot, as if he would have missed her.

Yet she who was identical to he
had grown alarmed when he first raised the curtain
on his obsessions, all the mad possessions,
that he had laboured to withhold from her.
What did it matter if his friend aver
her beauty or authority to judge
the same as he, that troubled him so much.
Why did he wish to save her from exposure
to his own doings, which in life they touch
as if in death, no closure overmuch.

And so it was for him she took the bullet,
although he were the only one to feel it.
Darkness prevails, but somewhere it is bright,
and somewhere his friend thinks of her tonight.

Ben Mazer

A NIGHT IN CLAREMONT

When the wind goes down, and with it night
surrounds the elementary, fantastic gardens—
idling a moment in recess from the crowd
by Byzantine fountains studded with night jasmine—
your talk of Shakespeare burdens deciduous leaves
trembling the shadows where I wait
for variants with sterner variation,
peppering the icteous footstep's pause.
Blown through with visitorious tremulations—
veritably keen, they publish a rumored text
long caught among the leaves, the horns and bramble—
I wait it out, drinking the air's shrinkage.
My old reprobate of blasts and Stambouls,
carries a sorry cane. For him night's gin,
but I am young as any promises,
colliding with the imperious speculum.

Gethsemane

You were insane, and I was sane,
now you are sane, and I'm insane.
I met you first in Gethsemane
when you are gone, and I remain.

The gardens there were lightly flush
at introduction of your blush
the kissing shadows nightly touch
time shadows render from the flesh.

The very bushes seemed to move
with attitudes approaching love
at the last moment to reprove
as if they didn't want enough.

Where earlier entering the town
calm was embedded in reknown
(directly it descends from this
perfect betrayal of a kiss).

The stirring petal on the bush
ignited by the kiss of flesh
the fragrance stirring in the air
shimmering like a distant star
the evidence that you are there
though even now it seems so far.

When you are gone, we meet again
when like a shadow fame and name
are predictably the same.
Men view the son, the desert plain;
when you are gone, we meet again.

Deep Sleep without Reservations

In my dream, I returned to Harvard Square.
A night on my own. I wanted a good meal.
I went to where I had often gone before.
It might have been The Pheasant, but it wasn't.
I was the first in line inside the door.
Some other folks came in, were quickly seated.
I mentioned this, and was brought to a table
in the large dining room, not the exclusive
(which had been heightened like a pedestal).
Three haughty men were seated at my table.
I asked if I could possibly sit alone
(I noticed there were many empty tables).
I tried to read the menu, but I couldn't.
I had a lot of questions for the waiter.
I waited for him, but he never came.
The people who came after me were eating.
I pushed my books a foot away from me.
I caught someone's attention, and complained.
I was told they would be with me shortly,
a party coming in had to be seated.
A hundred kids in matching uniforms
of red and white, with red scarves at their necks.
The people who came after me were gone.
I was enraged, asked for the manager.
She focused her preoccupied attention.
I told her I had been there many times.
I had to meet my wife and mother-in-law.
Was it possible I could order now?
A waiter would be with me in a moment.
The new waiter brought an Asian family

to join me, said she'd be back in a moment.
The child was feeding an enormous dog
she held upon her lap, just like a baby.
Bottle of milk in hand, she opened its mouth.
There I saw an entire electronic switchboard
of knobs and dials and indicating screens.
The young thing was a vegetable, they explained.
I nodded, and tried not to be too horrified.
Once again I asked for a new table,
rather politely. Suspicious and sick of me,
they asked me to stand and wait while they prepared one.
They seemed quite busy, perhaps disorganized.
The hundred kids in scarves were being served.
I'd had enough, and gathered all my books.
They brought me others I had left behind
on other visits which I had forgotten.
There were so many, how could I carry them?
I tried to stuff my pockets with the papers
I seem to have left in a great trail behind me,
tattered bits of poems and telephone numbers
scattered everywhere. They brought me piles more books,
rare first editions, some books that were not mine;
some of these were multi-volume sets.
I found some others hidden behind a curtain,
where I recalled they sometimes had shown movies,
startled to realize how long ago that had been.
I saw the old projectionist hurrying forth
and disappear. I tried to pile the books
in both my arms, but they kept spilling out.
I got them balanced, and they led me out.

Just then, I saw that there were empty tables
in the daised and exclusive room.
In fact the entire restaurant was empty.
My hotel was across the street. I had ten minutes.
Couldn't I just order quickly, and be done with it?
They gave me a table. But now I had no menu.
All I wanted was a cornish hen,
something I'd had there time and time again.
I worried that they were remembering me.
Their manner now expressed extreme disdain,
as if they'd made their minds up to ignore me,
I was a particular class of mental patient.
I knew I wouldn't be going there again.
I woke to find I couldn't even breathe.

THE GLASS PIANO (2015)

Lupe Velez with a Baedeker: Irving Thalberg with a Cigar

The smoky candle end of time
declines. On the Rialto once.
With Lupe Velez. Prepared the crime.
But Irving's valet was no dunce.

Had seen Tirolean dances there
before. And though she was no whore.
Perhaps was hired by the state.
Yet would not scare. And knew no fate.

Time's thick castles ascend in piles,
the witnesses to countless mobs.
Each with intentions, torches, throbs.
Bequeath the coming dawn their wiles.

Yet Irving was not meant for this.
He books the first flight to the States.
He suffers to receive Lupe's kiss.
While all around the chorus prates.

There's something does not love a mime.
Tirolean castles built to scale.
There was a mob. There is no crime.
These modernisms sometimes fail.

ANDANTE

All is flux and change, Lucretius said.
These gardens are kept manicured. This bed
is cradled high among the well-trimmed trees
that branch off into shadows, and waver in the breeze.
Night spotlights young girls' impulses to flee
where drunken bushes have the best of me.
Familiar songs blare distantly one face,
yet there are others hidden, beneath the human race.
A dim potato sprouts beneath the soil.
At summer solstice we retire from toil,
and settling in among the verdant reach
of shapes and colors find, observance in the breach.
There is no one to tell us what to do.
The driven many emulate the few,
and tearing away memory like veils
report internally, the iconry of tales.
One leaves one's life, to instigate another.
He is no brother, she no longer mother.
The unimaginable at last comes true.
And there is nothing left, and nothing left to do.
The heart is still, admiring pink roses,
no longer shaken by years' monstrous doses.
Somewhere all begins again anew,
and there is nothing left, and nothing left to do.

Autumn Magazines

The falling leaves of autumn magazines
are framed by nature. Frost said you come too.
Your gowns and sandals crown your nakedness,
each season justifies all that you do.
The sidewalks spread out their appearances,
the towers and the gilding celebrate
the dates and calendars, commemorate,
and underneath it all there's only you.

Spread over the vast sinking town
Which winter makes seem half asleep
A bus begins its movement down
Across a bridge into the steep
Wide view of the familiar sights
The site of many rowdy nights
But now inhabitants have thinned
Discouraged by the winter wind
And one less one is in the world
Because our faith and will have curled
And folded on the mantel bare
To leave unborn without a care
One whom God's glory wanted there

Intimations

I

Rows of deserted mannequins
are capturements of sleep's desire
along the late night avenue
where the small wishes soon retire
in slanted shadows of the lights
that shade into the memory
of similar imagined nights
along some other destiny—
the perfumes, and the costume pearls,
the feathered hats, a cashmere shawl,
accoutrements of other girls,
all comb the speculative hall
of minor satisfactions sent
to heaven's darkened wonderment.

II

You see it from some other way,
perhaps adjoined to panes of ice
across some kitchen's verity,
who pay not the required price—
god's eye of anonymity
encinctured ocean passages
to fell sleep's closed eternity
and stifle darkness with a kiss ...
The shards of fragmented approach
will be swept up when giants come
all other years to swiftly broach
your simple, broad elysium—

and tender a swift word or smile
of stippled presences awhile.

III

This violet sort of calendar
scuttles desire which is sent
where the October winds concur
on every orphan exilement—
the muffled shoes beat down the street
to join each lofty ornament
that sizes sleepers up discrete
along each sullen bafflement;
each exiled casement of the sense
entinctures trinkets in the hand
to ask one perfect recompense,
one seedbed spread across the land
in sleep ... Now fold the newspaper,
all mythic quarries to aver.

IV

Then finally, swept into the slant
of closing wishes to decant
some semblance of the tablature
perennial only to the time
of crying eyes that glide the mirror
of steady junctures seized in rime ...
each signal imprint of pure form
upsets the census of the norm,

belies some craft's indifference …
Stand tall and striding thus framed hence
project some future to recall
the blistered marble of the sense,
and hang your hat up in the hall,
one integer and protocol.

I shall not need your arms in heaven,
nor gem-light singular of your eyes,
before I come to six or seven,
to lure me with much keener lies.

I shall not need your legs in heaven,
you dangled bonny by my side,
but forward all things shall be riven,
eternity we shall abide.

I shall not use your eyes in heaven,
to steer me forth into the sun,
but as when conversation's done,
shall be unto the darkness given.

The poet does his finest work in sin,
travelling across the world to kill his love,
real beauty's on the outside looking in,
at what each year spring to the pollen does,
at tides of granite whirling to new cause,
new steadiments aligning to new pause,
but love is heated by the same old sun,
true beauty's on the outside looking in.
The noon's bazaar, with hazing to be won,
indifference to how each customer ticks,
they flood the streets of Sydney, or are done
with dust for cafe by the blow of six,
the main thing is protect the potato bin,
on this assignment, outside looking in.

Suppose she falters, crushed between the hand
like paper that a flame extinguishes,
let rice and poppies blow across the land
to sing her praises, buried with the fishes,
time's truth is darkness, and the dark is vicious,
even poets must confess their sin,
observing Christmas dinner from the bushes,
a pas de trois, and outside looking in.
The punts of April chafe Ophelia,
pierced by a silver Buddha on a pin;
who splits the spectrum will contrive to steal you;
and though no greater beauty come again,
and blaze like towers while the absent spin,
let God himself be outside looking in.

Ben Mazer

When she is lying in her grave,
no other men will know what silence gave
to the wind waving all the tops of trees,
to the snow falling on the empty seas,
how she in silence would surmise
eternal death that lurked behind men's eyes,
how words would seize
the visages of memory that flees;
she is so still, that lying there
myself am prone to utter disrepair
to have loved, and seen my true love flown
to silences that I have never known,
to distances where all is reconvened,
not shattered by time's heartless lying fiend.

And now each place I walk like one who's dead,
surveying the scene where this or that took place,
this ghost beside me, this familiar head,
will bob awhile, then vanish without a trace.
And I am not the things I thought I was,
because the one who held me in esteem
has taken away effect, removing cause,
till all is vanished, someone else's dream.
There is no labyrinth can take me back
to magnetisms that had held in place
the centered world of all that I now lack,
who long once more to look upon her face.
And I am cast in dark eternally,
and live, but shall no longer live to see.

Gradually the house across the way
grew dimmer and brighter, appreciating the stars,
as languidly dropped the words they would have it say,
long in the lucubrations of new lovers,
who sat outside, all hours of the night,
to watch the seasons pass and sense the feelings
of being, divinity untangled from the light
squeezed by the tabula rasa of its ceilings.
Gradually, grown troubled and vexed by poison,
that could not go unnoticed or unencountered,
the fiend undid the gossamer thread of reason,
and the whole season panicked as it floundered.
Desperate with disappointment she duly countered,
breaking her pact with the sun, and moon, and stars.
Tried without sentence, the heavenly funeral biers
shed disapproval crashing where they sauntered.
Now she goes, alone with her cats and fancies.
Her final word has dealt them a fatal blow.
No more of dances, dresses, or of chances.
And God has folded up to see them go.
Then as he changed, for each was forlorn and broken,
he marvelled at the fierceness of her reply,
that she should truly wish to let them die,
saving no shred or scrap of any token,
and their flush season never more go spoken.
The school yard and the flowers and the grasses,
averted their eyes to prospect such cold shrinkage,
now never more each stranger here who passes,
will ponder the eternities of perfect linkage.

To see her face cracked out with frantic horror,
you would be broken too at calm so crippled,
to know there isn't any more tomorrow,
just two cats, sullen and indifferently nippled.
Yet there they lie, prostrate, without recourses,
ploughing the winds of empty solitudes,
not knowing to what degree to feel remorses,
or savour the absence of their finer moods.
No more the bagpipes breathing through the city,
the peopled monuments now all unclaimed
by joyous chatter, eaten up by pity,
no more the great love which was duly famed.
She, one supposes, now has been retired
to simple acts, to duties and to sleep,
while his lot is incognizably mired
in the immense unanswerable deep.

THE PLACE

That was the place where once they stood,
incognizant of things done well,
of things that come to any good,
immune to heaven and to hell.
How well they knew each breeze of it,
each leaf, each rock, each branch, each crack
that future generations lack,
nor know that they were part of it.
And yet the summer nights would drop
eternal manna on their heads
just fifty yards from where their beds
held them who came to a full stop.
And yet the long spring afternoons
had stirred with hopes of private things,
that even the poet never sings,
till love itself had come to ruins.

WINNIE'S TOWER

Autumn afternoons, between the hours
that time is strictly helpless to impose,
young Winnie takes me up into his towers,
and what is far becomes exceeding close.
The wind's indifference rustles leaves of gold,
and dust puts a pale film upon the air,
Winnie says we're young when we are old,
sensing the ones who were before us there.
Ah, in childhood only the wind troubles desire
on days like these, when all comes to a stop,
but Winnie says that we shall never tire,
dreaming of other lives from his tower top.
Old ivy climbs the tower till it reaches
our revery in which the world seems bare
of all the insignificant, dormant breaches
that intimate to subtle hearts their care.
And though I linger, not ready to go home,
the ghosts of my own former lives will come,
waiting for night, and the full moon to rise,
for we have made such reservations with the skies.

He sauntered briskly on the tennis court,
and stunned the matrons with his supple play,
to whom he proffered all his coy asides,
to stimulate each calyx as he may;
his need was great, though he had well concealed
the origins of all his worldly prowess,
the requisite of his eccentric field
attendance to the summer's bridal showers;
he noted how his daughter, fully grown,
had taken after his peculiar ways,
who made a little fortune of her own,
observing that his method always pays,
his plan to move them to the countryside,
where now the whole expanded clan abide.

The Glass Piano

Unfamiliar and incognizant
flat shadows dense oppose expanding time
light scurries there, essence prismatic blent,—
myriad and marmoreal paradigm ...
come into focus, and demanding light!
night's clockless teleology of sight
assumes no history, but of wall's stoppage
and window's leakage flowers that are savage
ravage and rack and blight
some lost pearl harbour in the dead of night.
The bombs explode! Just so the glass piano,
which lies so still and patient in the hall,
the predicate of morning—bright Diana!—
lends harmonies to evocate the all.
Leaves flutter—why should they not?—reclaiming space
that scenes are cast in—who could not remember
the absolute interment of motion in place
where heart abided in some lost September?
The crowded episodes dry thunder havocs,
light dimming until old memories are unblind
with ritual escapades, exodus stratospherics,
redeem all distance, portents of the mind.
The hours they live in, empty shells, adornments
of simple wishes, mornings of coffee with friends,
project in violet visages their torrents
of supple lucidity where mind unbends.
They travel far—were distance not an illusion—
only to return, wearier, wiser,
a momentary stay against confusion,

heaped in vast relics absence solidifies there.
How can they be upheaved?—the droll bell drones
them whole again, lacking space to confine them,
as if some Europe sauntered to their homes
to rise again, to which the dead shall bind them.
The mind shall settle thus, in slim beliefs
exonerated by its supplication
to static roots, the true note of creation
falling blankly as spent and fluttering leaves.

To look at them, who moved so easily
between the garden or the railway station,
who sat for hours where the boats came in,
with little movements fused in unity,
as if each were a breeze jostling the other,
drinking their coffee, talking of next to nothing,
could one perceive what brought these two together,
firm in their bond through any kind of weather?
Now that their endless conversation's done,
the morning cigarettes, and seaside sun,
the fairs, the city days, the nights alone,
who is there to pardon or condone
the reasons such a two should be as one,
or make a world out of the observations
they shared through all their many incarnations,
or break the existence of their summer dinners,
or other such bright realities disperse?
A cat might notice: lace curtained unities
of street and tree, long pregnant nights in winter,
of rainy days through all their perorations;
but what is there left to give the faintest hint
or evidence that these two did exist?
Now they are done, by whom shall they be missed?

The idle roofs are slags and crags
of chunks against a mildewed sky;
the weight of human history sags,
and rain ensnares eternity.

The mind absorbs the present's waste,
and stumbles forth with humble haste;
no human heart for miles around
is gleaned or makes the slightest sound.

The night comes on. Enveloping rain
ameliorates the glow of pain,
that grows, although its face is numb,
and all its origins are dumb.

Turn in the car lot; spin around;
electric lights without a sound
shed color and a point of view:
man circles, nothing left to do.

Go, make your midnight pilgrimage there:
the empty lot, the empty square,
fall back into some sleeper's dream,
and have no elemental theme.

THE GOLDEN PEAR

for Ivan Kustura

Nowhere are shadows swept more tall nor deep
as where in the walkways of the midnight hour
the long low friends move slowly, as if to steep
God's own unconsciousness with inner power,
silently blazoned where their memories keep
cool casements resonant of summer's tower,
talkless where richnesses have yet to weep.
Turn then, and face away; eternity
shall never again make any room for these
poor figures, stuck in their dream of happiness
richer than any kingdom or provinces,
and keep your eyes, though there be nothing left to see.

When like a perjured idiot I ran
into the calling of my great despair,
I tried to speak, but could not heed my care,
until in ruin lay all I began
ten thousand nights ago in my great need
beneath the lordly green catalpa tree
that steadied me, whose steady anchor freed
the steady years to my great potency,
the gossamer-threaded scene of ecstasy
where timeless I queried the divinity
as to the substance of what I must be,
and worked the anvil of my force and creed;
thus dying thus, I saw before me fold
my charge, so absolute, I had been told.

I saw her once, I don't know where I was
or whether I dreamed, but she was so familiar
it was as if in life she spoke to me:

"You cured my life, and made me well again,
but after time I knew that I must leave you,
not because you lacked any success,
or qualities that make a woman love a man,
but because you strayed from me, because
something went wrong somewhere in your heart,
so when I spoke to you it was not you,
but someone in a fever of distraction
whose focus was entirely elsewhere,
and fearing for the oncoming of age,
I knew that I must act to save myself …

"It was the hardest thing I ever did
to let you go, to let go my own heart,
reasoning to save us both our happiness,
to sacrifice—as was my character—
myself to the liberty you seemed to need …"

Then I, as tears began to swell my eyes:
"If I had known, if I had woken up
from the great dream that crushed me in its vice,
I would have poured my heart out through my eyes
to ask forgiveness, and return to you …
No matter what I did, my own heart knew
all truth and beauty, all I knew of love,
had emanated from the source of you,

who was too lucky with his lot in life …
When God decreed that you should be my wife
I stumbled and I fell, not looking back
even to notice what I myself had done,
who wept more water than the seven seas
when you had left me speechless and alone …"

The restaurants were peopled once again,
as they had been in life; there was still time
for conversation and the little things
that seem so real they fill us with belief …

Then it was she did a peculiar thing:
she handed me a single tiny pearl,
and kissing me on the forehead like a child,
she spoke as if to speak for one last time:
"Take this, in time which you may recognize
is crowded inside, like angels on a pin,
with all the things we said, and all we were,
so tightly bound it never can unwind …
This relic, keep forever close to you,
that nothing is undone, and what we were
shall keep you whole for all eternity …"

She turned, though I expected to hear more,
some sign of life that could bring back the past,
and seemed entirely preoccupied
with something very distant that she saw …
Then I turned too, and clutching my small pearl,
looking to see what it was she saw,

but there was nothing there … Then she was gone …
I turned in long strides towards oblivion …
The night came on, and memory was extinguished …

I tried to find you in that surging mob
of people fleeing deasil-widdershins,
but swift eternity would never stop,
nor would god pardon any for his sins ...
All grew into a fervoured disrepair
of people tumbling every sort of way,
I searched the fog but couldn't see you there,
my lips were mumbling things I had to say ...
Was then I realized where I might have been,
struck by a ghost's familiarity,
the rags and market lanes of countless men
and women stretching far as I could see ...
All I'd forgotten came back in a flash,
strange places I had visited on earth,
known faces as I made my breathless dash,
imagination that preceded birth ...
I saw the lanterned gardens of old love,
of places I had never even been,
all indistinct as memory's treasure trove
of what the heart keeps silently within ...
Was then I realized I was truly lost,
in scenes without beginning, without end,
and reckoned the immensity of cost,
of loving you, of having had a friend ...

THIRTIES POEM

To love you I have to carry a spear in my hand,
roast a pig and a pineapple on a spit,
go diving for pearls, telegraph by wireless
the coast guard and mainland that we aren't coming home.
Naked we channel the loop of a waterfall,
breathless and coming up drenched and shaking our heads,
counting the stars and the lights of the ships at sea,
one utterance, of scurrying officers monotony.
How many flights like this one has modern man
archetypally repeated in Tangiers or Turkestan,
one voice in the wilderness, swimming and making a plan,
waking in morning to pearls in a coffee can.

NECESSE EST PERSTARE?

Twenty minutes after midnight. The houses sleep.
And in them the tales of ships, of clocks, of houses.
The tales of voyages, and the return to houses.
One after another,
one next to another, or attached to each other,
their different shapes, or same shapes,
bigger, smaller. Longer, wider. Taller windows. Shorter
        windows.
Loud and crowded, or empty and silent,
with a telephone, a car in the driveway or out front,
and places to sleep.
You walk out (if you are him)
into the October evening at a brisk pace
with a newspaper tucked under the arm of your Harris tweed
looking about chiefly at wind
blowing dried leaves blue white brown
into or out of ditches or onto trees
till they're a little wet,
it is true.
But you and I, we meet in rain,
where we can come in from the rain,
and have a sandwich, and a coffee.
They telephone each other,
on regal steps, fast and alert.
From one to another, string trees with lanterns,
to God above, the son of an old love.
Morning. The leg swings forward long and wide.
Mariana Pineda is no longer trapped inside.
A Columbia student now, eyes roam the brick facade
of an apartment building, in the land of Nod.

Keystone cornices replace the God.
A son of the Alhambra declines to pack a rod.
A generation, scarred by ghosts of war,
meets on street corners, each greeting as before.
The whole great mix has been to the theatre,
read the papers, interrogated the interlocutor,
in closets with incense, in kitchens with bathtub whiskey,
B. G. Brooks, Zoe Hawley, Viola Tree.
Up drives with radios, in uniform,
to telephones, each waiting for the forum
to isolate with definition their indecorum;
they greet on corners, in guttural voices, ailing,
jolly, with teeth and uteruses failing.
And speak one language, good for spring canoeing,
after long winters of Napoleonic rueing.
Necesse est perstare? This too will come,
later in summer to most, in spring to some.
The college widow deftly sidesteps a bomb.
The student union sounds the general alarm.
There is no lack of things to look and see,
of books to read, of points to ABC.
Only the still window, in the unwitnessed hall,
must be susceptible to anything at all.
And will greet guests, in winter and in fall.
Each couple knowing the same modern dances,
and how the judeo-christian world enhances
the pagan rituals and rites of spring
the voice trapped in a gramophone must sing.

Cracked faces, aligned in a vacant ring.

Ben Mazer

Cracked faces, to battle ancient come:
brick buildings rise to God—a vacant emporium.
While trains rush out into the provinces—
old ghosts the armour in the hall commences.

AN AFTER DINNER SLEEP

Entering the open air summer movie theatre,
the hour after dinner, the sky grown dim,
some rustling heads bobbing to find their seats,
the lights come on the screen, the show begins,
displacing cares and attitudes of the day,
each one prepared for a personal fantasy,
the sudden change of scene, and you are in
Cairo, privy to an intimate conversation,
silence broken by the crackling of spoken words,
clipped and conspiratorial, lush in its ease,
settling down to a world of eternity,
where all repeats, and is forever there,
unchanging, after many a crowd, many a show,
to which the people nightly come and go,
leaving them there, these conversationalists
who never change, but dissemble unattached
in the cosmos as light and sound, electric charges
of being constituting their own drama,
vanishing in space but not in mind,
reminding us of the nature of our being.

Movies are ghosts that couldn't get around.
Trapped in a ray of light, a wave of sound,
a box of tubes, molecular ghosts flee
conditions atmospheric that surround
continuums of time and entity,
broadcast indentures of God's parity,
stirring the memory they feebly hound
with words and images that aren't there,
their afterglow that is so tightly wound

141

around the lurch and flux of stratosphere,
forgotten to be remembered where they stood,
parti-esoteric where most good
as individual fuel to meditate
the chasms of existence which abate.

Walk into the theatre five minutes late,
and hear the voices as you find your seat;
look up and you are in a photoplay,
a drawing room in Cairo or in Crete,
mid-conversation; catch the words they say,
their brittle echo through the theatre,
and settle in for a two-hour stay,
and try to understand what they aver:
they speak so fast, then dry, deliberate,
where missing walls extend out to the sky,
the dry hump of a hothouse crescent moon,
the wall-less proxy, the old family friend
who's always there when things begin or end,
wherefore his great need to be involved?
The panic of your dreams is slowly solved,
to sample dramas that extend elsewhere
to hieroglyphic myths with rumbling hair ...
You hide the nazi, or you turn him in,
to let the ancient rituals begin,
Tiresias, who has foresuffered all,
a poster selling popcorn on the wall ...
A bat will hover in the drawing room,
and orient the audience to doom

they might escape, but they will wait and see
the zeitgeist tested for alacrity ...

then file out to their domesticity.

Out of the fog a certain voice is thrust,
like clip clop footsteps hovering over feet,
the opening audio of a photoplay,
where you come in to follow as you must,
Egyptian nights of aristocracy,
tapping their cigarettes against a case,
the close-up crackling of a newspaper,
an intimacy to which you defer,
relishing summer palms on winter nights,
like men who disappear into a club,
out of the fog into a library,
where silence is so thick that you can see
maidens undressing in silk negligees,
or exports on their landwards way to sea,
invisible interests in the provinces,
and fall to a dreaming after-dinner sleep.
The mountains thunder, and the seas are deep,
drenched with the images of ancient worlds,
a Chinese emperor's hospitality,
on the eve of travels, the profligacy
of fields of poppies, saffron, cardamom,
all threatened by the revolutionary bomb.
The shards of images, blistering, torturing
the mind, have left the Hampstead evening blind,
though turn into an alley as you might,

imposing doorways return you to your sight,
firm as the grave, brass knockers that confer
fragments of fear and peace where the rats stir,
until a voice awakens, "Good evening, sir."

Now the two sisters have returned to London.
If one is done, the other must be undone.
You strain your eyes through columns, chance to see
the early return of the Viscount-Marquis.
Your monthly pension takes you on a spree
to Biarritz, Bretagne, Brittany,
and you will not be back till early fall,
and then again might not return at all,
the garish drainpipes climbing up facades
all violently symbolic, and at odds
with simple pleasures countrysides bequeath
to girls with dandelions between their teeth.
There is no fiction that can firmly hold
the world afloat above the weight of gold,
but all your progress drains out to the lee
of million-fold eternal unity.

What is the charm of slippers to the stars,
the hammering rumble of the Hamilcars,
projecting all their mysteries to see
the chimney-pots spread out across the city,
and the slow box of incremental fires
merge kisses on the operatic stairs,
hidden so that even time can't see
the mumbling promises you made to me.

I read all night, my eye falls on the door
in silent shadows at the stroke of four.
The nymphs have left stray shawls upon the shore,
who urgently into the cabs had climbed,
in softer hours when brief love still rhymed.
Who shall unlock the eternal paradigm?

Laughter streams like rain across the cars,
stirs audibly the let out theatres,
where no other form of silence mars
the peace of ribboned letters thrust in drawers.
The ibis is in concord with the rain,
mosaic rivers, remote and Byzantine,
relieve the world, lift childhood from its pain,
whose process multiplies its fertile sign:
how to brick buildings the whole world can fall,
as if it never happened, as if all
had gathered in this room to gently sleep,
incognizant of promises to keep.
And whosoever shall redeem the squalls,
each rivulet which from the dark sky falls?

Germ sprung from a rock, a windy castle
returns to earth. The dry grass strains the wind
of cooling planets, a headless knight, germane
to April flowers springing from dry earth,
their numbers countless as air-flight manifests
that dot a century, Centurion.
This German seed of proto-indices,
atomic memory and stark component

145

of motion and of glottal utterances,
folds lightning in the ocean, breaks the mountains.
Not strictly grey or brown, the cardinal
exhumes slim shades of green that break the earth.
Seeds fly through air, and taper like a ghost
among the querulous, germinal and moist,
the apparitions of old savoire faire.
A windy springing, germinal, germane,
to monstrous waves washed on the wasted plain.
Tall waves of blade-whirl take all men again
as Hokusai envisioned, turned to rain.
Erected castles, bilious suburban gain
the poet's eye sweeps in his lofty pain,
travelling far above the orphaned roofs,
no vocable but the component grain
to settle all the sleepers in his proofs,
component vocable that can't be split
where all dramatic situations sit.
Our German is the philologic core
of indic madness, mystery, and more.
Germ sprung from rock, a windy Elsinore.

One cannot assess the force that drives the rain,
if driving thus into the heart of pain
the recent past endows a partial stain
on the whole present. Crosswinds cannot solve
what crowds that drift into the rain revolve
around the present, too soon to resolve
the forces extant, thoughts the wind sprang
up to serve humanity from culture's cup

the dying light on which the victors sup.
Nothing sheds nothing. Whole particular
world cognizances suffer to aver
the wind wrought eyes the rain will wet and blur,
too soon too late. We are not what we were!
While god alone will scale and fill us up.

Unreality is not pushed back,
but like a fiction emerges, unreferenced
except in qualities or sense-data,
unverifiable in their own closed systems.
This is enough to posit they are true,
or in some sense neither true nor false,
but welcome enough, for their indications.
Take for example two ends of a street,
from one end which (and which end is it really)
out of the London fog our man emerges,
a complex of unbound hallucinations,
of uncompleted bearings or desires
that can't account for outside precedence.
Why should the dream not murder the real man,
or seem to do so, if but fractionally,
as if to say I've read of it what I can,
when there's no reader but in lucubrations.

A brown fog wraps as it will seem to do
around the armchair and the lofty view,
with yellow light that penetrates the ceilings
uncertain of its basis in the feelings,

but focused on a yellow text of page
that rises up in Sanskrit to the age
of Lanman's Harvard Oriental Series
and modern philosophic notes and queries.
How wide the margins, blocking from all view
all but the virgin snows of Waterloo,
the type like armour standing in the hall
that makes you think of anything at all,
where disconnected from October night,
dead through dead branches vacant wind takes flight,
germane anticipation of the snows
to which all speculation surely goes,
firm and abrupt as the Hapsburg empire
finds only vacant agents left to sire.
An after-dinner dream! Surely to sleep
the Buddha's fire sermon falls so deep
it is not wakened by the telephone,
or windy castles, or a vacant bone,
but stands evaporate in the March air,
germinal, not counting any there,
and speeds across the rooftops of the village,
in search of ideal innocence to pillage.

A rare edition floundered in its state,
the words dreamed over fed the seven seas
with passages, the cosmos conjugate,
bereft and baffled, of disparate entities ...
Dr. Cyriax sitting on the bridge,
who counts the lights go out, obstructs a star
from sinking to her cabin, very far

from where the last transmission throws its switch ...
These others in their beds prepare for dawn,
but in the streets the London fog goes on,
past ceilings higher than the eyes can see,
reflexive light of pure staticity ...
The Dr. is impressed with what we learn,
and counts the distant panels as they burn ...

Before you awaken into consciousness,
you may have some vague memory of this:
a garden, loosely bounded, in the sun,
to which the archer and the gardener come,
a statue of Cromwell standing undisturbed,
inhuman innocence that's unperturbed;
and you may meet Goliath in the shed,
among the worms disturbing the frost's bed.
A sundial tells you all you need to know:
of vital noon, a barrow, and a spade,
a berry-laden bush bristling in shade,
the calendars old apparitions made,
where galaxies of dust are lightly laid
on shelves while all are sleeping, and the maid
has not materialized this morning yet,
where wars of memory settle till they're set
in night's cool meditations, a penny ante bet.
How can we climb to see the latest show,
the silence Europe's soaked with what we know,
the ravaged Orient that bursts to blow?
We lay in beds, and watch the headlights pass
along the walls, across the frame of glass

that covers up a clown's face, painted rose,
through depths of living which each person knows.

Symphonic dull varieties of green
animating with a classic spleen
each dangling berry focusing the scene,
the chessboard motives of inhuman voice
simplifying the surrounding noise
of splashing youths with allegoric choice,
the trireme of the sun, the wind, the sheen
of rippling image, one fondly silent threne,
while Socrates, philosopher no more,
almost historian, stands at the door
of webs and teacups, lyric fantasies
that draw the crowd to scaled eternities ...
attention to the situation, scene
of every choice transformed by what has been ...

1940s Middlebury symphonic clown
green green green green green
swirl the trees by the luscious pool
tympani breezes rotswort towering
shaved limbs conductor affixes
to Plato and caves and frames
Socrates famous for saying hello
masturbating in the center of the meadow
while night sleeps in slithering marble
occasionally a passing headlight's glow
but there is no philosophy here
but only

the tapping before the orchestra begins
and the bathers in their emerald tight skins
who know from an accent that you have come a distance.

Webster transposed to an attic. Orange alcove glows.
A tree leans. Light sweeps its leaves
like wind or rain. The window lets in a little view.
How we hump and toss our memories
in comfort there. Silence like talk flows,
tossed by the wind or rain, swept by the light,
tossed cool. An ancient stage direction stirs
a bit of speech, jumbled in modern tongue.
What do we wait for? Who are we waiting for?
In torpor languishing like wind or rain
we toss our memories. A bit of speech stirs,
breaking the silence, and correcting rain,
as if to say, "I was expecting you."
So much to think. So much to do.
The city spreads out various from here,
adjacent to our seclusion's wider sphere.

Sudden appearance: that's epiphany.
A world that comes from nowhere is the world.
Slinking around corners along the sidewalk squares,
in mornings that are oblivion: that's the world.
They come to our attention: nubs of twisted steel
lovers maneuver around. Are they us?
Are they us to be so large and fill the world:
inceptions which are immense: eternity.
The mind blocks out so much, that it can see.

Then rain comes, punishing the evening roofs,
and hurrying progress, so blind and inert.
A cab's closed door—prelude, a change of scene.
The downpour buries lovers in their love:
slinking away to what has never been.

No recollection in the art nouveau wood
stirs them to action; a roof of trees inside
their ingrown sickness is enough and good
for clatter of teacups; some may feign to hide,
fooling themselves, but not go unobserved
by doctors' rushing inactivity,
the least of hope, that justice will be served,
doubting their secrecy's insanity.
Some recognize a mother, or a sister,
returning to threats of doctors' cruelty,
their unburst fears to carry like a blister,
their nemesis personal continuity.
For to know fraud, cures of the charlatans,
have stood at doors, on beaches more than once,
thinking escape must mean the fatal pounce,
as diagnoses slip through traitors' hands.

Go back to that day. The shadows thick
with seeing by the Chanford Arms.
The colors brilliant as a day in May.
Our eyes alert as if we had been sick,
noticed inscriptions carved into the brick.
Easy and voluble, slow to make our way,

we set out, and although we richly dreamed,
we never dreamed that we would come to harms.
We were preoccupied with how things seemed,
and how their seeming, broken into bits,
made up life's flux in all its starts and fits.
We talked your childhood out a country mile.
Night: twentieth-century man in a turnstile,
recording images, marking the blurs of form
that keep each in his solitude from the storm;
we passed beneath the windows thickly lit
with fleeting scenes, that were the whole of it:
the whole of man, alone, and quite unknown,
scenes never changing, though the years be gone.
Happy to be as brilliant as two stars
that soared above the earth, and looking down
at all the tinkling lights of homes and cars,
in voices booming as the Hamilcars
remarked ourselves, then gently turned towards home.
By-passing every strict familiar sight
and obverse of the odyssey of night.
The gallery of unalterable fires.
Lit up, yes, but in the end quite slight.

He looked around and saw what he liked best,
and he prepared his own Octoberfest.
The winds were grey, which blew like billowed clouds,
beneath which he discerned among the crowds,
the missing forms of many lit-up shrouds:
a grocer helpful in Thanksgiving rain,
a wall street banker waiting for the train.

Ben Mazer

The headlines of the newspapers averred
a unified delight in the deferred
long hour of homecoming. All were heading home:
by days, and hours, changes at railway stations,
out to the provinces, with a little patience.
He closed his book, and leaned back in his seat,
and saw the thousand images repeat.
For him there never could be going home.
There was the eucharist. There was the poem.

DECEMBER POEMS (2016)

Among my Harriets I find
(Ah, you see I am not blind!)
one, disdaining, au courant—
savage bibliophile, douxieme partant.
I do not think that I could walk like her.
But leave it to others to aver
when the wind comes sailing down with an October frizzle
as others through windows shall be left to touch
these calendars we thumb through overmuch,
to changes you can touch down to your shoe
mid traffic out on Euclid Avenue.
I thumb their contents, but shall leave behind
withal a firm impression in the mind
of what it is to find
after so many fires have burned to ashes
the thumb that's restlessly moved over the latches
of surprise, as if an act of being kind
could change one's mind.
But burning cheeks, departing with a whistle,
in Joliet could not write such an epistle
as Harriet, nor such a missile.

EPITHALAMION

A wedding in the house of Frankenstein.
A thousand tapers rising to the ceiling.
Victor tells his bride what's yours is mine.
Dressed in white satin she is most appealing.

The maids are standing waiting in a row,
and drink champagne as they are bid to do
by the old patriarch, who straightens a flower petal before he go
to think dynastic thoughts, as men incline to.

Some thought the devil planted in his head
an aeon ago, somewhere alive and breathing,
wings homeward to upset the marriage bed,
and wreak hell's havoc till the town is seething.

How could philosophy assert a rift
in happiness that any man would treasure,
grown independent of his eccentric leisure,
stinging the early promise of his gift?

How could he give life to one as one,
and not as twain or twin, before his time,
and not expect this out of wedlock son
the sacred bridal chamber wall to climb?

The monster must be chased to the old mill.
Parade of doom, ten thousand burning torches.
The evil shall be purged by good men's will.
The creature thinks, parental absence scorches.

While Victor thinks, I've killed the thing I love,
displeased my mentor, and the lord above.
I doubt he'll be returning to his books.
I cried myself, but gave no dirty looks.

FROM "December Poems"

VI
Christmas Lights

The car lights turn and probe the wilderness
of Christmas carols sung in the abyss.
A bill board flashes, roadside bars flash by,
forks in the road, a half glimpsed library,
and here and there between the thick set trees
bright lights of peaceful domesticities.
The world's a place! Car hurtling through space,
record each image trailing 'cross the eyes,
as brief and tender as your lover's face,
signs like lone voices that a side light blurries.
We climb the slow climb to the Christmas bed,
as vintage words rise from each vintage head,
and lie down in the crystal dark awhile,
pillows, blankets, comforters in a pile,
and stare across the way to see the trees,
those strange divisions of eternities.

XIII

Angels come and go from room to room,
who know the attributes of each great year,
ideas' condition, and what is held most dear,
on a mischievous whim, who may even grab a broom!
They come look in on us to see we're good,
not fallen in the muddle of our making,
the alert pressures of our fate are breaking,
we are not fallen where we loved and stood.

What is their interest in such refinements
as cannot cogitate another soul,
but filled with toil at the allowed confinements,
should let a second prisoner out of jail?
I thrust my calendar into the hail
of stoic winter, and am good for bail.

And how do the mystical divisionists
segment off to what's never found again,
the high, obtuse dust tower of the pen,
the quibble drawn and quartered on the mists
of evening rooms, and providential feasts,
invisible to time, yet there lives fire
intenser than the focus of the choir,
and all is urgent, just because it lives,
and in the mirror, life to life life gives.
The full bird song will grow soon in the trees.

Yet there's a band that goes through at nine o'clock,
restless to stir the summer into being,
because one night to meet each will undock,
and each in love be crystalline for seeing.

XV

Your long thin hands are warm and free
and dust of snow blows from the tree
that focuses the wind and light
from the far away of a winter night.

It seems to blow from the North Pole,
touch many an individual soul
in wooded houses far away,
where other lives and people stay.

But we are snowed in in the dark
when everyone is fast asleep
and all the world seems bare and stark
and buried in fresh snow very deep.

We light a candle, and surmise
the wonder in our gleaming eyes,
cast into an eternity
of love's bright lonely sympathy.

XX

Old love, when all is gone you will appear
and hover about my bed. Our conversation
will have the freshness of another year,
and stir old fire with each exhalation,
as one by one death's trains depart the station.
"Love, I was faithful. Filled with adoration
and wonder at the fact of your creation."
"I panicked, and at my first fears I flew.
I didn't realize what I'd done to you."
"But we were so in love. Remember, heart,
we knew that we could never be apart.
I, for my part, was too insensitive,
when there was so much more I had to give.
Forgiveness is not needed any more.
For time has closed the partly open door."
"It is not true! My ghost exhumes your ghost,
and in eternity we are not lost!"
The words come late. So many tears we've wept,
here in this very bed where we once slept.
"Remember me! Love, let me back to stay.
Heart, hold me tight, and don't abandon me!"
What might have been is lost to speculation.
Our bodies have been broken of sensation.
The time has come to put our love away,
to be forgotten for eternity.

XXI

The gold flames rose above the rooftops,
new life rests powder blue on the facades
of morning's silent tenements, and the past
is weeping in the shrubbery, falling fast.

What illness havocs, what's there of forgiveness?
The children play within the unkempt impulse
to write your missive, or to throw away
the whole of it into a paper basket.

The tiger comes in spring, illogical
finally to the senses. But of man
and woman, put away the spring
from which wrath pooled. Conclusion has been fooled.

At last your eyes can focus on the distance,
and take a more reserved and balanced stance,
free of the pains that time will put away,
the attic toys left for another day.

Night will come, with fish in newspapers,
crowds rushing to and fro, the butcher's scale
a momentary respite when the sale
of memory shall reach the monstrous whale

upheaving cities with its massive tail.
There will be time for weeping at the window.
Progress will cease at last, for life is slow.
And there is nothing that you do not know.

XXII

I see all now. I see that all was splayed,
and crystalline and perfumed as it swayed
in shadowed gardens, high up in the air,
and in the sheeted windows what's not there.

This was the birth of love, the cracked and clear
strange perpetuity unreaching here.
The fountains fountain, and they must continue
when I can no longer lose or win you.

We slept together up above the world.
Experience had to the surface hurled
its words. Now all is past and streaky grey
of what the gods had rendered for display.

What of forgiveness? How bad must they hurt
to break all trust, imagine the faithless flirt?
Of resources in common that they had?
How to forgive the lover who goes mad?

Gigantic flowers sprout where our love seeds.
Larger than all the predicted deeds
we might have done. Satanic death has won.
How then to extricate one from but one?

The senselessness is senseless above all.
The accusations have begun to pall,
and are not there. Some other goes instead,
to walk deaf, mute, and blind among the dead.
Yet just last week you told me a good story.
You must have ducked while entering the dory.

Yes, what of forgiveness? Is there rest in peace?
Lately I had wondered why disease
should take you away again, beyond my call.
Man has no needs, none looking over all.

My dear, they cannot say you were unfair.
Last time I held you, you were hardly there.
Magnificent your future, without doubt.
Now that your benefactor is cast out.

But I shall love you as you truly were,
and speak no more to others to aver
the softness of the rain that's made of mothers.
Not I, who never knew the love of brothers.
I must have abused you when I sat and gazed
upon your beauty, and was hardly phased.

They sit there, listening 'round the radio,
those in the photographs I didn't know.
Are you there? Like a speck I understood
were all the nights you proffered me your good.
The Christmas lights shine briskly all the year.
I will not take them down till you are here.

XXV

My wife is sleeping beautifully alone,
under the moonlight, skin and rib and bone,
my lovely treasure, going without pleasure;
I weep beneath the covers with a phone,
in case she wakes with nightmares; I'd rejoice
to waken in the night and hear her voice.
I myself am scared to go to bed,
and hold the covers tightly to my head,
calling her voice in murmurs and in whispers,
weeping a long time till the silver sled
of sleep shall take me sliding into dreams
where all is mixed up badly with what seems,
or isn't, till I wake with fear and panic;
while she lies beautiful and epiphanic.

Start with the rain. The day starts with the rain.
The Sunday rain. Another Sunday rain.
Let it go on and on and on like pain.
Thus find your elemental theme in rain.
There is no business raining on the roofs,
and but one light that lights the horse's hoofs.
Low to the ground, sink into earth to strain
the music of the sky opening its vein.
Without a sound, but wind that whips the leaves
and hammering like fingers on the eaves,
the day begins, the luckless lover grieves
sinister mysteries the mind perplexes,
the lifeless throbbing of the dullest flexes.
So what has happened to another year?
The eye scales brick and stillness plumbs the ear,
and there is no one there to truly hear.
The calendar with love has been cast out.
The vows and promises another route
have taken, not what might have been.
The soul is empty underneath the skin,
the faithless lover lies in naked sin.
Just so. With rain you let the day begin.

The streets are slick with memory's reflections,
the many byways of the mind's directions,
wet thick on brick,
where nothing in its mystery shall stick,
affording a proper end to introspections
that have no name, where no two are the same,
except in the unity of your dissections,

the fame of the eternity's ejections.
Mankind is sick.
And comes up against naught but stone and brick,
not certain what there is he should atone for,
or what there is that he should truly moan for,
is there some reason that he is alone for.
He's quite insane, yet know him by his name
and you shall know the most and least of pain,
the troubles he has opening the door,
what stretches forward, and what comes before.
There is nothing holding you together,
except the windy and the rainy weather.
Then turn the corner, you shall find there's more.

Now for the story of the childhood kitchen,
the glass panes that tall skies and bare trees look in.
The highest branches whip in puzzling patterns,
the eye spins in, with orioles and terns,
from our perspective like a broken chalice,
the snow lies bloody just outside the palace.
The bowl steams, operatic in precision,
the child staves off the moment of decision.
The wind will whip, and snow melts on the ground,
at night the diggings of the silver hound,
elemental in his spiky collar,
from door to door his howling ghostly holler.
But here is safety, all well understood,
the mother symbol of maternal good.
Spaghetti swims with unity's division,
and history is a preempted vision,

171

original, and scarcely known to one,
who finds this day the world has just begun.

Chaplin appears, the first time he is seen,
revealing flickerings of what has been,
and Caligari, tortured in oblong angles,
beer garden, mental institute, who mangles
memory. There is a lot to see
in first encountered shards of history.
After awhile the branches blue and thicken
with winter darkness, stillnesses that quicken
the senses, and an orange light comes on,
a single flare that signifies day's gone.

FEBRUARY POEMS (2017)

The sun burns beauty, spins the world away,
though now you sleep in bed, another day
brisk on the sidewalk, in your camel coat,
in another city, wave goodbye from a boat,
or study in an archival library,
like Beethoven, and thought is prodigy.
Do not consume, like the flowers, time and air
or worm-soil, plantings buried in the spring,
presume over morning coffee I don't care,
neglect the ethereal life to life you bring.
O I would have you now, in all your glory,
the million-citied, Atlantic liner story
of what we were, would time come to forget
being so rich and passing, and yet not covet.

Hands that are old and are trivial, never be old
too much to remember these flashing scenes:
fainting in the parking lot on your wedding night,
the lawns of Claremont and their gossamer sheens;
the great joy, running away from the crowd,
to the celebratory and nuptial garden,
the twin exits where lovers disappear,
or the calm of breakfast, away from the strangers.
Hands that rest in my hands, what is a year
to the inexplicable, docent memory
of a thousand nights, and a thousand days,
Italian restaurants after the plays,
or the garland of flowers, dried and withered,
carried by hands to place on the graves.

The Living Angels

The living are angels, if we are the dead in life
and immaculate beauty requires discerning eyes
and to ask incessantly who you are
is both our strength and doubt in faith, to know
what we must appear within ourselves to know:
that we do love each other, that we know who each other is
by putting ourselves in the hands and the eyes of the other,
never questioning the danger that rides on words
if they should misstep and alter a logical truth,
or if they should signify more than they appear to,
whether dull, indifferent, passionate, deeply committed
or merely the embodiment of a passing mood,
some lack of faith in ourselves we attempt to realize
through the other who remains steadfast in all the flexibility
        of love.
Stay with me, speak with me, remain with me in silence
but remain with me, abide like a flame
enduring the terrors of the wick engulfing and sputtering
because I have made these declarations from a place like yours:
conceiving the only happiness in a chosen hope:
that love will be so because we want it to be.
Harrowing the lives of these angels who are so much like us,
we fail to see them in us, but they are there.
Apologies must harrow, too, wherever they falter
and mislead us, into the terrors of our separate doubts,
most at home in the pristine snow of each other's arms,
ceaselessly bounded back into the current of the tide
reverent of touch, its indelible yearning and lament
to which we apply a delicate balance of assents

with which to commemorate as much as through a flickering
of the eyes
the spirits, and shapes, and forms of our greater desire,
that which hangs with us as life in these angels on earth,
the bodying forth of the evaporate intrinsic self,
that which we put our faith in by taking hand into hand,
our more than faith, being studious of ourselves,
choosing not to live separately in one quandary
because the archangel of angels commands us in love.

Look, and see where these images of ourselves
beautifully depict with utmost sensitivity
our hopes for a better life, which lives in us,
which is the spirit at its essential and most transparent,
like Chaplin and the orphan peering around any ordinary
brick corner,
not smiling, though we must smile when we meet each other
over a distance, heading in one direction
because humour is our great joyous clue in life,
happy to be heedless, hearing music in the acceptance of
chaos,
where music is an appreciation of the aesthetic sense
that burns in us, delicate, discerning, and unique.
Fall not into the sea of total evaporation
that threatens to undermine us with its undertow
of doubt without reason, of reason without doubt,
knowing full well that even the living angels
must suffer a seachange only to remain constant
to that which they must be, even the dead in life,
that the highest reaches of our possible understanding

must attain to an iconry that will live without us,
because we have been on earth, and have truly loved.

Even Fred Astaire and Ginger Rogers, in Top Hat,
just before dancing cheek to cheek as true lovers are meant
    to do,
experienced the seemingly fatal setback
of a pure misunderstanding created by logical circumstances,
yet could not avoid the very real truth of how they felt,
so beautifully realized in a visible sheer grace of sharing,
itself mimicked by the tight movement of two moving
    together
effortlessly but with utmost joy in tact,
greater than the world itself a love such as this
which faces two together in its immaculate scope,
looming and large as any of the designs of God
for partners with a discerning sensitivity,
the highest realization of life whether in heaven or on earth.

We move through dusty streets, because dust moves with us,
being the dust of stars and the dust of heaven.
Listen how silence itself mirrors forth the greatest warmth in
    seeing,
smiling as again and again I take your hand,
like Chaplin or Keaton at the picture's end,
and that is the music of earth, and proper to angels.
It is haunting, this beauty, and returns us to us.
We are the visible windows of a darkened shop at night time
mirroring back to us images of ourselves.

The greatest joy known to mortal man,
shall live beyond us, in eternity.
Catching you ice skating in mid-motion,
cheeks flush, winter pristine in our hearts,
ineffable, permanent, nothing can abolish,
when the deep forest, buried in snow's white
holds the soul's eternal solitude,
when, melting coming in, each particular
that stirs the senses, is the flight of man
to unspoken urgencies, garrulous desire
continually fulfilled, the captured stances
that drift like music in the light-laced night,
shared words in murmurs soft as downy sky,
the stars observe with their immortal eye.
Furious, presto-forte homecoming
races into the eyes and fingertips,
confirming and commemorating bells
resounding with our vulnerable desire
in momentary triumph that's eternal.
Life passes on to life the raging stars,
resonances of undying light.
All years are pressed together in their light.

Useless, useless, the thousand memories,
shadows of trees whipping across the wall
in the luminescent shadow window,
too deep and early youth's fields of dandelions,
old heavily perfumed apartments in the rain,
drawers neat, commemorative matchbooks tucked away,
clean linen underneath the guest room bed.
What's real is so contemporary it's real,
you now in your youth, my beautiful wife,
the only thing I know that makes me laugh,
the only thing I know that makes me love;
how can the world boil down, distill to this,
two eyes shining, the flesh soft and alive,
chatter, and laughter, and wind, all that exists?

This breathing in my arms, that it should end,
be put away for an eternity,
is like a letter that we never send,
our souls that our own lovers never see.
Yet they see all, the shattered heart laid bare,
the long accumulation of despair,
the passion with which we express our need,
our joy at loving them, the day we're dead.
It chills me to be seeing my own ghost,
for just one last time to be playing host
to memories we carried through the years,
to hold you in my arms while my heart sears,
this breath that was mine an eternity,
before it's gone, along with love and pity.

Summer, the powder air, the longing trees,
the minstrels love and orphanhood,
drove us beyond the campfire to the wood,
where the thick pines would still the cooling breeze.
Our disguises kept us through a season,
the frontier circling the new century,
and no one thought to look for you or me,
so we lived simply and without a reason.
Ah, but the nights we sang in harmony
and pleased our brothers, cool beneath the moon,
each danced his own way, though we knew one tune,
yet we were hunted, and at liberty.
I often think with fondness of those days,
how much we loved, how innocence never pays.

Slat-light leaked the dawning of our love,
abrupt pickpocket, cool eyes in resolve
to see the mercy of the godly cove
stand in the doorway, hungry like a wolve.
We were reckless then, and yet we were
precise, meticulous, a savvy pair,
not squeamish to make a hot revolver purr,
or make forbidden waters our affair.
With ease we both kept coming back for more,
absurd routine, deceptions on our sleeve
contained our laughter, and we used the door
as both a place to come, a place to leave.
But then I caught you in my arms at last,
you never struggled, and I held you fast.

So many bridges crossed, as evening falls,
the famous curves which memory preserves,
one God-star of the brick and peopled thralls,
one raindrop radioed to eternity's walls
in multiple perspectives. Mankind calls
across dusk's echoing air, the thousand sights
that pass so quickly to our quiet nights,
newspaper, dinner, questioning our rights
to know the world, husbands and wives hurled
up to the stars' magenta light, such plights
around which every roadside bump is curled.
Know them again! and know them once for all,
the flashing signs, the vacant lots, the sprawl
and pall, precise as individual people.

Ben Mazer

Spring Equinox

Yet there's no malice, when you pine alone,
confused and paralyzed into resolve ...
Can only imagine secrets from yourself,
the wellspring of the buried memory,
what must be for the self to find no solace
in being loved, in loving in return
the man you asked for children, now gone mad
from wondering who you are, as if you know,
who cannot find yourself in anything;
they stand in ruins both, can love revive
the unity that's natural to them?
Or is some foreign obstacle, some sense
or lack of sense a disconnective force,
making oneself a stranger to oneself,
a stranger that emerges, known to none,
long years of happiness misunderstood,
and lingering where we left them in the fall?

Can anything resolve divided knowledge,
caresses rejected, but not lacking fire,
their proof the mad desire in the eyes,
itself sustaining night, the moon and stars,
as if without them they could not be real?
No reason for her fear can be explained
by anything but being; it's the same
with he who is her mirror, loving her,
though she can't see beyond her chosen walls
the impregnating power of the wills.
Does something come to break apart the fall,
make of it winter, something unforseen,

186

less true, misunderstanding one's own self,
to lay the glittering ornaments on the shelf,
and close the windowseat one final time?
Is there a something, which is quantified
by touching fingers to a less than being?
Is there at last, itself, an end to seeing?

These questions go unanswered, perplex and linger
as if you had not been yourself at all,
wearing the natural costume of desire
that can't be met, pacing the parapet
to no end, glorifying death by madness:
they seize desire nothing can snuff out,
because you have not yet been fully born,
but struggle in the womb of vast recall.
I stay with you through sickness, thick and thin,
a ghostly semblance of what I have been,
recovering disparate needs, identities,
that keep us apart, although we are the same,
forgetting history, damaging the heart.

Troubled by not knowing your own secret,
you scrawl a coded message to yourself,
in hidden shadows, you believe conviction,
although belief is falling through the floor,
not true to who you are, who you adore.
I wait then,
scrabbled by insatiable pains,
and watching through the window at the rains
for signs of life, here at the equinox.

Ben Mazer

THE BIRTH OF VENUS

To see her perfect, with her head-down hair
string thin like spring, and all
the Botticellian newness, laughter from despair,
you would not think her mad, for she
is not—
the height of wit her rambling disjointed talk
that's born of pain, her easy deference,
and beautiful her unrecorded gestures;
we sit alone in the posh restaurant
to have some coffee only, bread and butter,
where she confesses she would be my mother,
could I be born, I won't say born again
though something like it is the sense I mean:
were all the same, and we could be together,
the thing she hopes above all could be true;
for far too deep a fire do the living
examine love and wit, the noble twins
of memory that make our talk a treasure
unprecedented yet by anything
in heaven or hell, though this is surely heaven.

By night she's wilder, steering with abandon
sharp corners, radio roaring early jazz
wrought from our marriage, delicate concession,
abrupt, decisive, beauty taking wing:
we roar up Plympton St. to stop a moment,
just in time to hear Marc Vincenz read
a final poem, wave at a few familiars,
then shimmy out into the whole vast night,
leaving a few unsettled, wondering …

To Speak of Woe That Is in Marriage

She described it better than I could,
the vivid harrowments on which she'd brood,
the injustness of another scent,
in her delusions that I was hell-bent.
It was a problem. Nightly she'd accuse,
she'd chuck her cellphone, fly across the state,
unreachable until she would return;
separately we watched our marriage burn.
She thought I must have married her for hate,
and walked the city; I began to lose
my mind when she returned with a torn dress,
and made up stories. Later she'd confess
she thought I meant to kill her. The duress
was traumatizing. There was no relief
from paranoia. O my lovely wife,
we were so happy, were so filled with joy,
the day we married; at the marriage feast,
when you were crowned with roses; after vows,
we flew the altar. We began to whirl
and dance about the garden in a swirl
of disbelief and wonder, and the rose
thorns pricked the evening when we stood apart
and sank into the shadows, dearest heart.
You asked to have our family increased;
I wasn't listening to your deeper yearning.
My faith was shaken; wasn't it a test
to see if I preferred your ghosts the best?
I couldn't recognize half of the names
your diary listed; only a fool blames
man, god, or nature, when the serpent comes;

we lay in flames and watched our marriage burning.
If I had taken you it might have eased
your restless soul; now we are lost and turning.
You turned me out; our separation numbs
your faith; you say you won't come back to life,
remove my ring, and cease to be my wife.
I never saw two crazier in love;
I saw the serpent swallowing the dove;
you vacillate; we're miserable apart;
I beat my head and I begin to cry;
at four I write you that I want to die,
and black out dreaming that your tender heart
tenders a few soft words, to raze the world
so I can rest, arms round my pillow curled.

How easy it was, to stand and look at the stars
with a cigarette in the middle of the road
on a cold winter night, when life was ours,
and all was holy, together, warm, and good.
So blue—remembering the distant years
that fell away—the stars still where they stood,
with us after dinner, and no fears
so much as hinted at, yet all that flowed
away somewhere, lost but to memory
that itemizes all the things we see
and which can turn an after dinner walk
filled with rapid breathless timeless talk
into great pain, the opposite of gain,
and can betroth the opposite of growth.
I want to hug you again! I want to hug you again!
And feel the cold tears burn, and kiss your mouth.

Who among angels weeps to know you bare,
forlorn, where darkness hides your face,
from he who loves you, who without a trace
has wept himself, from whom you disappear,
not even standing by the wrought-iron grids
that spike the evening, where the chill winds fall
all over memory, and leaves like tears that pall
the imagination hit the skids
of empty pavement, breaking over all
invisibly embracing like a ghost
the wordlessness of suffering you host,
when he would give you all, would give you all?
Oh God, turn back the clock some little bit
to where all was joy, happiness, and wit.

At the Altar

The wedding was fantastically rich;
immediate family only; I would be his bitch ...
He watched the guests with pleasure in the garden;
we sank in shadows; I could feel him harden ...
I sit in an Episcopalian church,
and hear his voice as he exclaims and boasts
how I am like some certain branch of birch
that's good for whippings, then he smiles and coasts
out of the room, to darkness and the night ...
He sounds so happy that my soul takes fright;
his friends are famous ghosts, all famous ghosts.
But how can you argue with a famous ghost
when he's possessed; I take the Eucharist,
scared by the watching nun, the smiling priest,
and see Christ's holy robes of purple blood
rippling and rising past my widowhood,
and weeping outside fall into the mud
as all the holy pass me going home;
my mind is racing, and it wants to roam
back to New Haven, thoughts not making sense ...
is Hell a women's center? Far away
the nuns are watching while the children play
with jacks like crucifixes at St. Mary's,
my alma mater that I have displaced
with His decisions; always trust in Ken's
uncanny stares that fix you with incisions;
O my God, to be a piece of wood ...
He spoke more nonsense, but I understood ...
I thought I heard him say I was a chicken ...
He thinks I'm just another of his chickens ...

Roast me in Hell; and this is life on earth ...
I whisper in his ear that I'll give birth
to Satan; the Birth of Satan, that's a laugh ...
He won't be happy till I'm sawed in half
and Satan's Son is fished out on a spike ...
My mirror looks like just another dyke
for him to plug; each Satan is a thug ...
He smiles and pisses coffee on the rug
for me to clean, while he goes out to fuck ...
O Mary, Mary, help me, I am stuck;
O Mary, Mary, I am out of luck ...
Will Mary marry Jesus, and then suck
my brain out of his ass, and kiss his muck?
Christ the Impaler has you on the floor,
spits on the walls, and motors out the door ...
I'm dizzy, London Bridge is falling down ...
He married me to be His maid and clown ...
I am his whore for life, His Sunday clown ...
There is no one in the world can frown
a frown like His; escapes are all shot down ...
O Mary, my experience has shown ...
but you can't hear me; Satan's being blown.
Life comes from mud; I lie in it and cry.
O Jesus, Mary, how I want to die ...
The bricks are falling, I am falling in ...
Tall buildings, glass and brick, can't save my skin ...
The bells are breaking, and I'm falling in ...
O Jesus, Mary, how I want to die ...

Fantasy of Kenyon College from inside McLean Hospital

The flowers are out in May, but I can't pay
respect to flowers from my locked in window.
A blurry postcard of symphonic trees
flurries in all directions from the breeze,
a thousand shades of green from bright to dull,
dull silver-greens and auburn-sapphire greens,
the long forgotten memory of queens,
and I am focused on the bricked in hull
of little white and brick houses, which cull
the finest students, meditative, silent.
There is nothing left I can repent,
but being here, fizzled, frazzled, feeble, spent,
unable to traverse my greatest wishes.
Aquarium window of sparse human fishes!
Two weeks and I will step into the sun,
the loveliest days of all the year all gone,
emerge into a world that's fresh and green with flowers,
hope to redeem the long stream's salient powers,
tar and molasses on a Carib isle,
see you again, and break into a smile.

Ben Mazer

After the show, the multiple streets go
on to their penny anonymity,
unfurl before the famous sights you know,
or disappear where human eyes can't see.
The little trinkets of the lone boudoir
will rattle in the silence of God's jaw,
as you will finger the invisible scar,
eyes heavenward with pleading and with awe.
Crushingly immense, the modern city
will have its way with loves, with lives, desire
seldom the equal of immortal pity,
and phoenix-like in incandescent fire.
Here stay me with a gesture or a look,
some few words torn out from some poetry book.

They sit among the brown pods dried in autumn,
upon the steps beneath the chestnut tree,
and count the stars and moonbeams that they see,
where wishes lurk in darkness at the bottom.
A look of scorn, a conversation torn
by fragile increments, true hearts beat mad
to insubstantiate all that they had;
the finery of wishes has been worn,
and shall not plague again these two's desires,
who peer out on the elemental fires
and curse their luck. God, will love come unstuck
and save these twain, who hurt themselves for fools,
or will the years on downwards further truck
with glassy love that in the shorn eye pools?

UNCOLLECTED POEMS

A Poem

When no one wanted to show they wanted it
it wasn't taken up, until it reached
one in a group on the periphery
unlikely enough to spark some jealousy
when she asserted with her true forte
not only her desire but just the right
tone and demeanor fitted to the part:
she moulded herself to it and history
so perfectly those damp lit misty nights
of silhouettes and neighboring beacon lights
she most chose to do her reflecting in
with one close friend unrended by the rain
are still the bane of her biographers
who felt she snubbed them once upon the concourse;
but she was only doing as she pleased
in saying the thing that had been there to say
by any of them before she came to stay.

TAKING IN THE CHANCELLOR

The chancellor will sip a bit of tea
then when he speaks up come straight to the point,
properly nodding with his face to the dark,
his elbow a perfect v over tea.
He wants to spend more time, just him and me,
pool data, a true topography of the city.
He knows that this work will interest me,
and he doesn't care how I do it. All his means
are at my disposal. There are no deadlines.
He wants to show me his new magnolia tree,
shipped from China. We sit in near shadow,
in conversation wicked to the core.
Only I entertain the chancellor.

The Girl

The girl I mirdered has a blonde white head.
De girl I mudered has no blond wite head.
Sher hath no little falsies any mur.
She no leg like a boa constrictor
or tight pin clip on a March fence.
She hath wondred hence
withouth a heade lake the sunflowre
or mouth ur powre.

THE WORLD

"The world will tell you when you're ready."
The world already knows you when you get there.
Aura of secret knowledge. When you're right
you'll help other people make the right decision.
But what that is no one musn't say.
Capture it on film, without telling the people.
Even the Guggenheim makes guggenheims.
The Guggenheim makes little guggenheims
until they're ready. No one is ever ready.
No one can tell you who the devil is.
Or knows who personally knows the devil.
I say you're right. Nothing's misunderstood.
People are geniuses who recognize
incipient genius, long after it's happened.
How can they understand what I've invented?
It's true, all the remotest galaxies
burned long ago, only the scientists
are fully present.

Mrs. Carruthers

Mrs. Carruthers
was not like the others.

In the red tent
they came and went.

Many nights
of streaked blurry lights

emotions like granite
wept from the planet.

Laughter before Darkness

2.39. The General's bedtime.
Summer glides low along the roads
out where a generator stops and crickets
outspeak the rush of leaves in the trees.
Behind thick glass, a prism of sounds retakes
a room a room has let onto.
A smell of soap parlays the entrance.
Now he is at command. The thin shadows
succumb to his vision, but not the sounds.
They shine like light into his consciousness.
Each decision he makes filters the internal television
of his contacts and liaisons. Rest
is what is needed, thinned to dust.

Land's End

The broad outlines shrink and descend
into the grotto where at land's end
the many pallored wait by the wall
of night blooming jasmine to recall
the terms of kisses and of promises
that no one misses fading to a turn
of honey briars where the shadows burn
an evanescent moment at the last
resort the present breaks into the past.

What have they become, do they remain
to bury there until the morning plane,
exhibits of headlines that are stellar
until the last keg smashes through the cellar
and reconfigured as Christmas lights
blend Hollywood with Honolulu nights
till the dreamt flights hang from them like pearls
amid an ocean of a thousand girls,
what is it that they whisper in the ear
as if at last their meaning could come near.

Ben Mazer

Wrong for Years

I wish to inveigle my way
into English society.
The lure of the Oxford chair
reaches farther than County Clare.
Another Oxford Don
has visited and gone.
The river of books rolls past
the socially miscast.
Forgotten unborn refrain
unknowingly insane.
From Dorset to Buckinghamshire
expire and then inquire.
Need not be greatly felt
but meaningly misspelt.
Return to go away
incomprehensibly.

A FORCE

Two girls—blondes; one was Scotch and one was English.
Fans of a famous writer who was singleish.
They followed him, although he never noticed.
Too young to see, or he had had to protest.
They found out where he lived, and staked him out.
Surprised at who they saw come in and out,
they thought that they would come to his assistance.
Cluelessly they worked for the resistance.
After awhile these blackguards all unravel.
Young girls don't write their memoirs when they travel.
They nailed him good, and then they turned him over.
You could have pricked the novelist with clover.
"You mean to say you followed me?" he said.
But he'll be stuck with one till he is dead.
She has his secret (though he is no jerk).
Besides she'll be a great help to his work.

Ben Mazer

FURIOSO I

I think that I'm a ghost in classical times
and that some other poet strums and rhymes
telling my story. I am an ornament
upon a rich man's lawn. I love your smile
that spreads through marble and is heaven sent,
strangely inhuman, and not what I meant
when I wrote my great ode, The Crocodile.
You huff and laugh and glower for awhile,
but I am shrunken, and my back is bent,
and will not enter where the solstice tent
confabulates the virgin's candid bile
where coolies with their baskets mile by mile
give no appointment, cede no sentiment,
and all that glimmers starward is on trial.

Furioso II

I think that I'm a ghost in antiquity
and that some poet strums and sings a ditty
about my life. I'm a lawn ornament
half-regretted by some rich man. But your lips
are as the quivering of the marble's hips
and lifelessly assent
to my one ode, and my last lament.
Your blush a mouthless totem, I am spent,
the youth I was concealed within myself,
nor bother any longer now with stealth
some paces from the palatial solstice tent,
go unacknowledged by the icy glare
of the sacrificial virgin there,
piled on the table with the lordly fare
carried for miles and miles by caravans
as black as night, trees' faces, circumstance.

Ben Mazer

A Star is Born

Her feigned indifference stung his vanity;
a small town girl with sawdust in her veins;
a modern pilgrim, who had changed her name;
a girl with glasses, thrumming in his brain;

the brazen hypocrite, she knew his name;
subscribed to *Star and Screen,* jumped out of cakes;
yet she had got his goat; he hit the brakes,
but felt his life was founded on a lie.

Big parties were his own familiar waters;
life took his coat; his name was on its lips;
he spent the evening in the servants' quarters,
trying to get a date, and washing cups.

He told the boss he wanted a screen test;
the studio would write him a blank check;
he told her that she never would be his,
that now she never could be like the rest.

His will was done; the out of town reviews
killed the first rushes, but the biggest news
was that her presence had eclipsed his fame;
each questionaire was filled out with her name.

Now in the afternoons when she came back
he had prepared a cozy little snack,
and they let down their hair; he didn't dare
tell her his fears, but she knew what they were.

He slapped a reporter, not the thing to do
when he had credit nowhere in the town,
except among the elder set who knew
just what it was the younger man had done.

Then finally left on his own holiday.
Prepared the picnic, but forgot the brunch.
He dropped his robe and swam out to the stars;
now you can see which one of them is hers.

THE GHOST

Why must you pace like that? You'll wreck the place
and I won't clean it this time. You'll have to.
This is the ghost then, which we always joked
in bed would come to haunt one of us. You—
you haven't really got it all together
and seem to have fallen into a deep funk
between the Coleridge and the china.
When I left here you said you had a plan,
you'd reached a new conception of your work,
but it's amazing how things never change.
The furniture is still where I arranged it.
I see us squirming in that one small room,
you working just as when I last rolled over.
Why is it we could never get along?
You always said you'd change if I would change.
But nothing has changed. Does the island change?
Stop pulling faces. Quit your carrying on
like Lon Chaney Sr. or John Barrymore—
wanting your orange juice served to you just so
or quiet while you look over the mail.
Granted you loved me more than anyone.

A DEACONESS

How about this distempered evenness:
deranged and lovely. The deaconess,
our traveler,
pity me to bicycle west. The best
time I ever had was with you. Who
else could have handled the preacher
as easily as you, his first teacher.
I am writing you because this
is the first chance I've had to miss
going to the bottom of having met you,
while you are on your bicycle now I bet you.

Ben Mazer

It's 9.30 in London town,
the long hand of the clock points down,
the little ones are in their beds,
adults receive on telephone,
the wicked lie alone in bed,
the phantom Draculas align
the boulevards upon the rain.
A shutter lifts the half of love,
the glory which has all to give,
the poison petals spread the sill,
the cream Magnolia in May
in urgent shadows unguent.
The faery hour builds to fall
like coke dust on the villagers,
or for the singular lover stars
become objective single stars.

Somnambulist Ballad

after Lorca

Green wind, erasing sleep.
Green branches, eroding dreams.
A ship far out at sea
and a horse up in the mountains.
Sawing the shadow
of her waist in half,
moonlight dreams on the balcony,
her face green, long hair green,
eyes ashen as the moon.
Skin green as translucent film,
face green as my long last look,
eyes a dull and flashing silver
colorless, without emotion,
meaning nothing, spent in the landscape.
She cannot see.
Beneath the primitive moon
everything watches.

The call is for warmth,
the hunt is for death.
Her face as tenuous and dead as green,
promising nothing, past recompense.
Charged with the landscape, bulleting questions
at the end of dreaming. My own death.

Vacuous and green
vacuously green
transparent without thought
spread across the night

like a translucent thread
where a small pine that moves
is mirroring his thought.
The horn it signals warmth.
The hunt it signals death.

Green, how much I want you, green.
Huge stars of white ice
with the salmon of darkness
come in dawn's river.
A tree rubs the wind
with sandpaper branches.
The cat of the mountain
bristles in darkness.
From where will it come?
How will it happen?
She lingers on her balcony,
green skin, hair streaming green,
dreaming of death and the sea.

—Friend, let me trade
my purse for your glass,
my horse for your house,
my knife for your bed …
May it be heavy iron.
Friend, I am bleeding,
I've ridden a long way.
—I wish I could, old friend,
accommodate your need.
But I am not more I

than this house is my house.
—How much worse the past seems in this light.
The wind signaling with its dewlaps, with its hassocks.
Hyper proximity of the hyper legal
always heading first for wherever you are,
the Bogart of gossip, the Dietrich of murder.
Old faces too familiar
no protection against the wind.
Figures of smoke in a landscape,
my first fears. A fullness
of words, ripeness in ruin.
Friend, I want to die
peacefully here with you,
and wake up in fine Holland.
The wind comes a long way from him
with its district of birds.
A maze of mirrors in which
I look not knowing which
is the true shard that moves.
Friend, can you not see
horrors no words can say.
Hide me in your house.
Let me die in my sleep.
Can you not see the wound
circling my heart and throat.
—Your stainless record shows us
two dozen bouquets of roses.
Your blood swims in your clothes
in a disarming pose.
But I am no more I,

nor is my house my house.
What was no longer is.
—Let me at least climb to the top,
beneath the spire, where I passed many hours.
Let me at least climb up
to the high balconies:
Take me there! Take me there!
to the green balconies
where I can see the moon and the sea.

Now the two friends go up
to the high balconies
shedding their steps of blood
letting their light of kiss
blurring the light with tears.
Dropping blood on each step
leaving trails of their eyes.
On some invisible roofs
a few trembling lanterns burned.
A thousand chimes were taking
the long hill in the dawn.
Green! I want you green,
green face, skin of green,
green gazes, bark of green,
sap green.

The two friends rose.
The large wind left
a dry, stiff taste
of mint and bile,

a strong, strange taste
of mint, sweet basil and bile.
Friend! Tell me, where is she,
your bitter girl?
How often she waited
how often she would wait
dark as the wind
cold as the moon,
on this balcony!

On the face of the water
cupped by the shore
she swam and swayed.
A green face. Long hair of green.
Glance fast as silver bullets.
—a fragment of moon
dangles over water.
Water revives
old memories.
Green as my chances, green
as the rushing band. Reprise
warm as a calling horn.
The shifting instruments
rearranging hearts. Time spins.
Life stops in a bar rest.
Night
becoming as intimate
as a small cafe,
as a village square.
Drunken murderers

pounding the floors.
Green, how much I want you green.
Green wind. Green branches.
The ship at sea.
The horse in the mountain.

Acknowledgements

The poems in this collection originally appeared in the following volumes: *White Cities* (Barbara Matteau Editions, 1995), *Poems* (Pen & Anvil Press, 2010), *January 2008* (Dark Sky Books, 2010), *New Poems* (Pen & Anvil Press, 2013), *The Glass Piano* (MadHat Press, 2015), *December Poems* (Pen & Anvil Press, 2016), and *February Poems* (Ilora Press, 2017). The section of Uncollected Poems collects for the first time poems which originally appeared in *Fulcrum, Salt, Horizon, Jacket, Agenda, Harvard Review, Zoland Poetry, Eyewear, Everyday Genius,* and *Flexipress.*

ABOUT THE AUTHOR

BEN MAZER was born in New York City in 1964, and educated at Harvard, where he studied with Seamus Heaney, and the Editorial Institute, Boston University, where his advisors were Christopher Ricks and Archie Burnett. His collections of poems include *White Cities* (Barbara Matteau Editions, 1995), *Poems* (The Pen & Anvil Press, 2010), *January 2008* (Dark Sky Books, 2010), *New Poems* (The Pen & Anvil Press, 2013). He is the editor of *The Collected Poems of John Crowe Ransom* (Un-Gyve Press, 2015), Hart Crane's *The Bridge: The Uncollected Version* (MadHat Press, 2015), *Selected Poems of Frederick Goddard Tuckerman* (Harvard University Press, 2010), and Landis Everson's *Everything Preserved: Poems 1955–2005* (Graywolf Press, 2006), which won the first Emily Dickinson Award from the Poetry Foundation. He lives in Cambridge, Massachusetts, and is the editor of *The Battersea Review*.